React Native for Mobile Development

Harness the Power of React Native to Create Stunning iOS and Android Applications

Second Edition

Akshat Paul
Abhishek Nalwaya

Apress®

React Native for Mobile Development

Akshat Paul
Gurgaon, Haryana, India

Abhishek Nalwaya
Jaipur, Rajasthan, India

ISBN-13 (pbk): 978-1-4842-4453-1
ISBN-13 (electronic): 978-1-4842-4454-8
https://doi.org/10.1007/978-1-4842-4454-8

Managing Director, Apress LLC: Welmoed Spahr
Acquisitions Editor: Louise Corrigan
Development Editor: James Markham
Coordinating Editor: Nancy Chen

Cover designed by eStudioCalamar

Cover image designed by Freepik (www.freepik.com)

Distributed to the book trade worldwide by Springer Science+Business Media New York, 233 Spring Street, 6th Floor, New York, NY 10013. Phone 1-800-SPRINGER, fax (201) 348-4505, e-mail orders-ny@springer-sbm.com, or visit www.springeronline.com. Apress Media, LLC is a California LLC and the sole member (owner) is Springer Science + Business Media Finance Inc (SSBM Finance Inc). SSBM Finance Inc is a **Delaware** corporation.

For information on translations, please e-mail rights@apress.com, or visit http://www.apress.com/rights-permissions.

Apress titles may be purchased in bulk for academic, corporate, or promotional use. eBook versions and licenses are also available for most titles. For more information, reference our Print and eBook Bulk Sales web page at http://www.apress.com/bulk-sales.

Any source code or other supplementary material referenced by the author in this book is available to readers on GitHub via the book's product page, located at www.apress.com/9781484244531. For more detailed information, please visit http://www.apress.com/source-code.

Printed on acid-free paper

Table of Contents

About the Authors

Akshat Paul is a software architect and author of the books *React Native for iOS Development* and *RubyMotion iOS Development Essentials*. He is also a seasoned technical reviewer for books on the topics of React, React Native, and Microservices with top publishers. He has extensive experience in DevOps, mobile, and Web development.

In other avatars, Akshat frequently speaks at conferences and meetups on various technologies. He was an invited speaker at the React Native Conference EU, Devops@scale Amsterdam, TheDevTheory Conference, RubyConfIndia, and the #inspect-RubyMotion Conference Brussels. He was also the keynote speaker at technology leadership events in Bangkok and Kuala Lumpur on TDD. Besides writing code, Akshat spends time with his family, is an avid reader, and is obsessive about healthy eating. More information about Akshat can be found at `https://www.akshatpaul.com/`.

Abhishek Nalwaya is the author of three books and has spoken at many conferences and meetups, such as RubyConf India and the RubyMotion conference. He has extensive experience in DevOps, Web, and mobile development. Besides programming, Abhishek loves to run and cook healthy food. More information about Abhishek can be found at `http://www.nalwaya.com/`.

About the Technical Reviewer

Alexander Chinedu Nnakwue has a background in mechanical engineering from the University of Ibadan in Nigeria and has been a front-end developer for more than three years working on both Web and mobile technologies. He also has experience as a technical author, writer, and reviewer. He enjoys programming for the web, and occasionally, you can also find him playing soccer. He was born in Benin City and is currently based in Lagos, Nigeria.

Acknowledgments

We would like to thank our families, who saw us through this book, talked things over, offered constructive feedback and provided support through our strenuous schedule without which conceiving this book wouldn't have been possible.

Also, we would like to thank Louise Corrigan, James Markham and the entire team at Apress. And especially Nancy Chen who gave us complete creative freedom to do things over the course of this book which some time took more time then expected. Writing a book is a long and arduous journey, but you all made it so easy for us.

Introduction

React is one of the most popular JavaScript framework as of 2019. It took web development by storm when first introduced and its popularity has been increasing among the developer community ever since.

React Native took this one step further when first introduced in 2015 and helped build Native iOS apps with common knowledge of web technologies like JavaScript. In just a few years, React Native has become an important player in native mobile development, and extending its support for both Apple iOS and Google Android was a game changer. This required us to write second edition of this book, which covers both platforms end to end to help you create stunning React Native apps.

This book is divided into ten chapters and each one teaches a unique aspect of building React Native applications. By end of this journey we believe you will be a master developer with React Native and will be able to publish your app to the Apple App Store or Google Play Store. We commence our journey with an introduction to React in Chapter 1, where you learn about core React concepts like Virtual DOM, one-way data flows, props, and state, and also build a small React application. In Chapter 2 we cover how to set up React Native and start building a simple Hello World program. This chapter also cover the anatomy of a React Native project and how to debug the application. In Chapter 3 we discuss design patterns like MVC, as well as new programming paradigms such as Flux and Redux. In this chapter you learn about Redux core concepts, how to use Redux with React Native, and the benefits of including it in a React Native application. Chapter 4 covers how to build a user interface (UI) with the help of Flexbox, navigation with React Navigation, and few critical UI components, such as touchable highlight, listview, scrollview, and more. In Chapter 5 we address how to implement device capabilities, including creating apps to use features like GeoLocation, MapView, Native Alert, WebView, and deep linking.

Chapter 6 covers a key feature that is essential to any real-world application: communication with back-end servers. In this chapter you learn how to make requests to get data from a server and post data back to a server using various available React Native options. In Chapter 7, we discuss how to access native application programming interfaces (APIs) that do not have a corresponding JavaScript library; this is building Native Bridge. This skill helps us harness all the features of native iOS and Android development. Chapter 8 covers how to write tests for our React Native application using Jest, and also introduces snapshot testing. This chapter also introduces a static type check commonly used in the React Native world, called Flow. In Chapter 9, once you have learned how to create a full-featured React Native application, it is equally important to test it with users and push it onto the Apple App Store and Google Play Store. This chapter describes how to beta test a React Native application with the distribution systems available for iOS and Android. We also cover how to create builds for iOS and Android, which is essential for submitting an application to the Apple App Store and Google Play Store. In the final chapter, Chapter 10, you learn about some popular React Native libraries and where to go next, how to get help, and how to stay in touch with the amazing React Native community.

In all, we hope that by end of this book you are confident in building your next mobile application with React Native and launching it for both iOS and Android. All the best!

CHAPTER 1

Learning the Basics: A Whistle-Stop Tour of React

The journey of a thousand miles begins with one step.

—Lao Tzu

Before you embark on your React Native journey, you must know a little bit about React (also known as ReactJS or React.js). In this chapter, we quickly look at the core concepts of React, which will help you to work on React Native. This chapter introduces the following topics:

- Introduction to React

- Virtual Document Object Model (DOM)

- One-way data flow

- React installation and setup

- Creating a first React Hello World app

- Introduction to components

- Props and state

Let's get started! React is different from most popular web technologies, and you will learn why as you move through this chapter. Its core concepts will open your mind to a new way of thinking if you have spent a considerable amount of time with traditional

© Akshat Paul and Abhishek Nalwaya 2019
A. Paul and A. Nalwaya, *React Native for Mobile Development*, https://doi.org/10.1007/978-1-4842-4454-8_1

frameworks; this new way of thinking is sometimes called *the React way of thinking*. You might have heard the phrase "Write once, run everywhere," but dismissed it as nearly impossible due to the explosion of different form factors (web, mobile, tablets). React has a different guiding principle: "Learn once, write anywhere." That seems quite different, and liberating. We begin this first chapter with a quick tour of React, which will help prepare you for React Native. If you have an elementary knowledge of React, you can skip this chapter and move on to Chapter 2.

According to the official documentation, React is a JavaScript (JS) library (not framework) for creating user interfaces (UIs). It was built in a combined effort by teams from Facebook and Instagram. React was first introduced to the world in 2013, and has taken it by storm, with community-wide acceptance and the benefit of being the technology at the heart of Facebook. According to official documentation, some consider React to be the V in a model-view-controller (MVC) framework, because React makes no assumptions about the rest of the technology stack used. You can use whatever technology you wish and you can create a single section of your app with React or React Native; you can also conveniently make changes in an already created application by incrementally adding React to it.

Why React?

Do we really need another JavaScript library in a world full of JavaScript libraries and frameworks? There is hardly a month that goes by without a new JavaScript framework introduced.

React came into existence because its creators were faced with a significant problem: how to build large applications in which data change frequently. This problem occurs in almost any real-world application and React was created from the ground up to solve it. As you know, many popular frameworks are MVC or model-view-wildcard (MV*), but here's a point to be noted and reiterated: React is not an MV* framework. It's a just a library for building composable UIs for UI components with data that change over time. Unlike popular JS frameworks, React does not use templates or Hypertext Markup Language (HTML) directives. React builds UIs by breaking the UI into many components. That's it, nothing else. This means that React uses the full features of programming languages to build and render views.

The following are some of the advantages of choosing React for your next project:

- *React uses JavaScript extensively*: Traditionally the views in HTML are separated from the functionality in JavaScript. With React, components are created and there is one monolithic section where JavaScript has intimate knowledge of your HTML.

- *Extendable and maintainable*: Components are formed by a unified markup with its view logic, which actually makes the UI easy to extend and maintain.

- *Virtual DOM*: React applications are blazing fast. The credit for this goes to the virtual DOM and its diffing algorithm.

- *One-way data flow*: Two-way data binding is a great idea, but in real-world applications it produces more pain than benefit. One of the common drawbacks with two-way data binding is that you have no idea how your data get updated. With one-way data flow, things are simple: You know exactly where data are mutating, which makes it easier to maintain and test your app.

To have a strong foundation with a new technology, it's necessary to understand its core concepts. The next section explores a few unique concepts of React, which will bring you one step closer to understanding this amazing technology.

Virtual DOM

In all web applications one of the most expensive operations from which an app suffers is mutating the DOM. To solve this problem, React maintains a virtual representation of the DOM (as shown in Figure 1-1), which is called Virtual DOM (VDOM). Along with a diffing algorithm, React is able to compute the data against the actual DOM and only update the part of the DOM that is changed. The amount of change is therefore less, which leads to a blazing fast application. In the beginning of your application you might not see it, but as your project balloons to greater complexity (which usually happens in real-world apps), you will begin to see the benefits of a snappy experience for users.

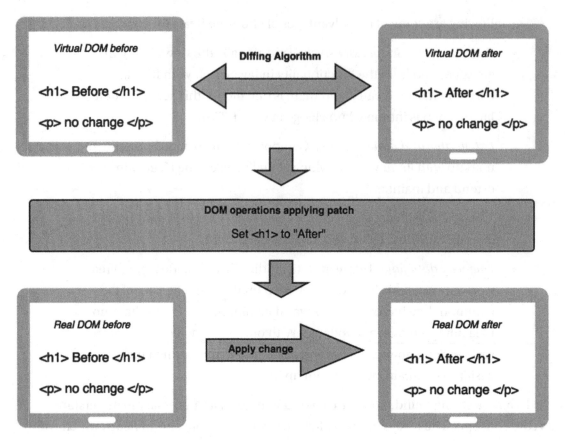

Figure 1-1. *Virtual DOM and diffing algorithm operations*

Manual DOM manipulation is messy, and keeping track of the previous state of the DOM is very hard. As shown in Figure 1-1, React solves this problem by keeping two copies of a VDOM. Next, a diffing algorithm is applied on these two VDOMs, which essentially checks for the changes that occurred and returns a stream of DOM operations. These DOM operations are then applied to the actual browser DOM.

Let's now understand in terms of components how a VDOM works. In React, every component has a state; this state is likely observable. Whenever there is a change in state, React essentially knows that this change requires a rerender. When the application state changes, it generates a new VTree; once again the diffing algorithm shares the DOM paths for required changes, as shown in Figure 1-2. This results in keeping manual DOM manipulation to a minimum.

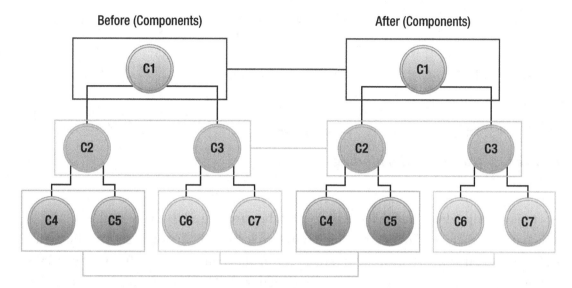

Figure 1-2. *Components with virtual VDOM*

This feature of VDOM is not just important, but a killer feature of React. DOM access is super slow, and honestly speaking, the world has made it worse by hitting the DOM again and again in most applications. To make your application fast, you should access the DOM as little as possible, and this is beautifully handled by the implementation of VDOM. You won't notice this with a small and trivial application, but once your app grows to include thousands of DOM elements all trying to get updated, React will not let your performance suffer.

One-Way Data Flow

React is primarily the V in an MVC pattern, but before you dive into the idea of one-way data flow in React, you must understand the challenges of MVC frameworks. One of the biggest challenges of an MVC framework is managing the view. As you know, the view component of the MVC framework is mainly the DOM representation. It is simple when you write code that interacts with the DOM, but it is very complicated for the framework to handle various DOM manipulations.

Traditional MVC views generally encompass a lot of heavy UI, and as the data change even for a tiny element, it eventually rerenders the app again, and the cycle continues. The reason for this is that typically most of these MVC frameworks follow two-way data binding (see Figure 1-3).

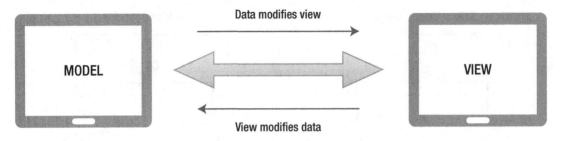

Figure 1-3. *Two-way data binding*

In JavaScript, data change in memory and they are bound to a view in the UI,
which means that when data are modified in JavaScript, which is in memory, the data
will be changed in the UI as well. In return, when data change in the UI (i.e., the DOM)
by clicking a button or any other event, they get updated in memory also, keeping
the two in sync. In theory, this works flawlessly and the idea is romantically perfect.
However, in real-world applications, problems arise when you have a fairly complex
and large application with multiple views representing data in one of your models.
As you add more models and more views, this two-way data binding ends up as
spaghetti with every change in data added to the pot, which sometimes even ends up
in an infinite event loop where one view updates a model, which in turn updates a
view, and so on, as shown in Figure 1-4.

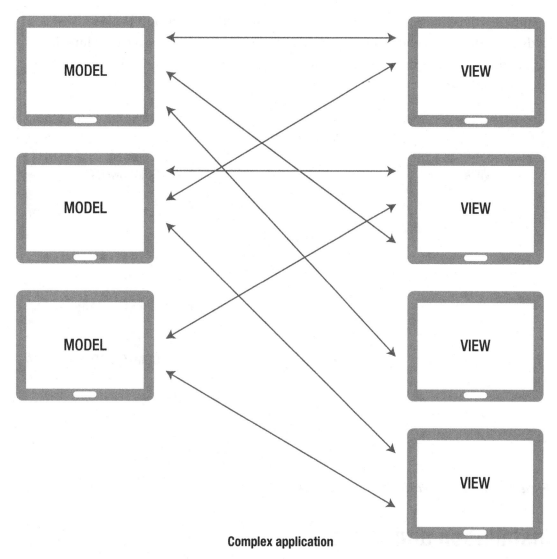

Complex application

Figure 1-4. *Unwanted spaghetti relationship*

Another issue with this system is that making changes comes at a very high cost. When you introduce a new developer to an application that is this complex, it's tough to understand the impact one change might have in this abyss of spaghetti relationships.

React follows one-way data flow to keep things simple, as shown in Figure 1-5. It is based on the concept of separation of concerns (SoC). This is a design principle in computer science in which an application or program is divided into distinct sections, each addressing a single or specific concern. The value of this design principle is that

7

it simplifies development to create a maintainable and scalable application. This leads to modularized code where an individual section can be reused, developed, and modified independently. This makes so much sense and is indeed an example of intelligent thinking.

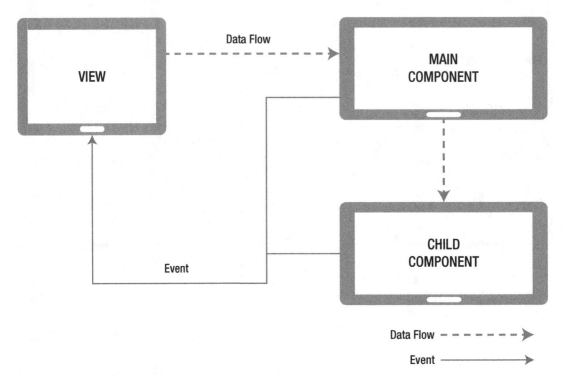

Figure 1-5. *React Native's one-way data flow*

Installation and Setup

To understand practical examples, you must first set up your environment to run your React code. Because React is just a node module, there are lot of different ways to set up a React project. We can include React in existing projects using npm or yarn and start using it. If you are starting a new project, we recommend using the create-react-app npm package. It is an out-of-the-box command-line interface (CLI) created by Facebook that creates a basic structure for the React app and takes care of ES7+ translation though Babel and Webpack. You don't need to focus on configuration; instead you can focus on writing React code. You can find more details about this module on its official npm page. If it interests you, you can also check its github repo from here to look at its documentation: https://www.npmjs.com/package/create-react-app.

For our purposes, we simply set it up for our development environment with the following command to install `create-react-app`:

```
npm install -g create-react-app
```

This command installs `create-react-app` globally.

Note   If you want to use the multiple-node version on the same machine, we can use nvm: `https://github.com/creationix/nvm`

Now that we have installed `create-react-app` globally, navigate to the directory where you want to create a project and run the following command:

```
create-react-app <application_name>
```

where `application name` is the desired name of the application. We need to use npm naming conventions, so the name should be in lowercase and cannot start with a dot or underscore.

We are all set to start working with React, but before we create our first app we recommend that you install React Developer Tools, a very useful Chrome extension that allows you to inspect the React component hierarchy in the Chrome browser. This tool can help boost your productivity. To install this extension, search for React Developer Tools in the Chrome app or open the following link in the Chrome browser:

```
https://chrome.google.com/webstore/detail/react-developer-tools/
fmkadmapgofadopljbjfkapdkoienihi
```

Create a Hello World Application

Now let's create a Hello World project. This command will install the essential packages and set up our React project.

```
> create-react-app hello-world
```

Running that command installs the dependencies needed to build your project, and it generates the initial project structure. Create React App installs the latest version of React and React-DOM, as well as the latest version of react-scripts, a development dependency that manages all other development dependencies that include starting, testing, and building your app. Create React App uses Webpack and Babel under the hood, but it generates only the files you need to work on your React project.

Traverse into the directory using your terminal or command prompt to play around with this application using the following commands:

```
cd hello-world
yarn start
```

It will automatically open http://localhost:3000/ in your default web browser and you can see the first page of our app.

yarn is a package manager like npm. It was created by Facebook and is the default that comes packaged with create-react-app. It is up to you to choose whether you want to use yarn or npm.

One of the advantages of yarn over npm is that npm always requires an Internet connection, whereas yarn can be used offline if you have installed it at some point in the past. Yarn is also very fast when it comes to package installations, which saves a lot of time in day-to-day development.

Introduction to Components

Components are the smallest units in React application development; they are indeed the most fundamental part of React. React is a library for building UIs and components are the key for creating any UI in React. You might think of it as widgets (like in Flutter) that you can plug in anywhere. These components define how DOM elements are created and how users can interact with them. The whole concept of components is that they are totally encapsulated, making them easy to test and reuse.

Creating reusable components is a work of art, and React provides many features for you. We will do a deep dive into them soon, but first let's open the hello world app we created.

Navigate to App.js in the project folder.

```
import React, { Component } from 'react';
import logo from './logo.svg';
import './App.css';
```

```
class App extends Component {
  render() {
    return (
      <div className="App">
        <header className="App-header">
          <img src={logo} className="App-logo" alt="logo" />
          <h1 className="App-title">Welcome to React</h1>
        </header>
        <p className="App-intro">
          To get started, edit <code>src/App.js</code> and save to reload.
        </p>
      </div>
    );
  }
}
export default App;
```

This is the main App component. As you can see, it's just a JavaScript file that contains some HTML code. If you have been building software for some time, you know it is a best practice to keep your HTML and JavaScript code separate. Looking at this example, it goes against this fundamental best practice. The reason this best practice exists is to decrease coupling and increase cohesion, which means we write the UI in HTML and logic in JavaScript. The challenge with this approach is that we can only attach behavior to HTML through HTML elements (like ID, class, etc.). A library like jQuery is a good example of this. As your files grow, it becomes difficult to manage and test your code. React components solve this problem very well.

It lets you create JavaScript objects using HTML syntax. Components serve two purposes: templates and display logic. Therefore, markup and code are tied together intimately. Display logic often is quite complex and to express it using template languages does become difficult. The best way to solve this problem is to generate HTML and components from JavaScript itself. React JSX solves these problems with its HTML-type syntax by creating React tree nodes.

Going back to the preceding code snippet, App is a JavaScript class that is inherited from the React Component class API. Components can be created in two ways: one using class and the other using function. Components created using function are also called stateless components. We discuss this in detail in later chapters.

The App class has a render function or method. As the name suggests, it is used for rendering of our content, JSX markup. render is always a pure function, which means it is immutable. It's like a single frame in a movie, as it represents the UI at a certain point in time. Updating the state inside a render will again call the render function, which once again, triggers render(), which then does the same thing, infinitely.

We are also importing Cascading Style Sheets (CSS) in the App component. Create React App uses Webpack, which takes care of importing CSS in the final bundle.

Now let's create a new component Message.js in the project folder and update it with the following code:

```
import React, { Component } from 'react';
class Message extends Component {
  render() {
    return (
      <div>
        Hello to React World
      </div>
    );
  }
}
export default Message;
```

Now, we can import the component into the main component App.js file and render it in the render method with the following code:

```
import React, { Component } from 'react';
import Message from './Message';

class App extends Component {
  render() {
    return (
      <Message />
    );
  }
}

export default App;
```

Now browse `http://localhost:3000/`, as shown in Figure 1-6.

Figure 1-6. *Browsing for the default message*

Before we dive deeper into this component, let's create a component using the functional approach:

```
import React, { Component } from 'react';

const StatelessComponent = () => (
 <div> Hello to StatelessComponent </div>
);

export default StatelessComponent;
```

This is the preferred way of creating a component if your state is not changing. It eliminates the class-related extra code like extends And constructors and makes the code more testable.

Deep-Dive into Components

In this section, we explore the vital concepts of components, which will help you work with them easily. We will learn about `Props` and `State`, which help manage the flow of data or state. The `Props` and `State` objects have one important difference. Inside a class component, the `State` object can be changed, whereas the `Props` object cannot. Now let's take a deeper look into both `Props` and `State`.

Properties

Props is simply shorthand for properties. Props are how components talk to each other and the data flow is immutable. Props are passed down the component tree from parent to children and vice versa. One key point to remember is that props cannot be mutated when referenced from a parent component.

Let's update our Hello World example to use props. Open `App.js` and add the following line:

```
<Message text="Hello to React World"  />
```

Here we are initializing the `Message` component with a prop named `text`. Let's update the `Message` component to display the text:

```
import React, { Component } from 'react';

class Message extends Component {
  render() {
    return (
      <div>
        {this.props.text}
      </div>
    );
  }
}

export default Message;
```

If you refresh your browser, you will see a message from the property for your inner HTML.

As your application grows, you need to make sure your components are correctly created in the first place. In the case of a property, you can specify a kind of property with a range of validators. This ensures and validates the kind of data received. Let's take look at this by updating our Hello World example. The `Message` components that we created accept prop text, so this string will always be required to render a `Message` component. Let's update our `Message` component.

```
import React, { Component } from 'react';
import PropTypes from 'prop-types';

class Message extends Component {
  render() {
    return (
      <div>
        {this.props.text}
```

```
    </div>
  );
  }
}
```

```
Message.propTypes = {
  text: PropTypes.string.isRequired
};
export default Message;
```

Now to test this, go to `App.js` and temporarily remove prop from `Message`:

```
<Message />
```

Now check the console log in your browser, as shown in Figure 1-7.

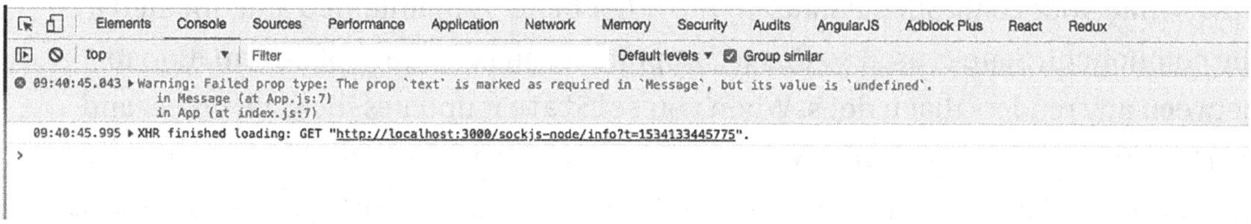

Figure 1-7. *Checking the console log*

Prop validation is a great module that can help developers to hunt down bugs. Here, the `propType` keyword signifies a hash of prop names and their types.

There are many other property types. Note that you can add `isRequired` to the end of any `propType` to make it required.

```
//some specific JS primitive
  optionalArray: PropTypes.array,
  optionalBool: PropTypes.bool,
  optionalFunc: PropTypes.func,
  optionalNumber: PropTypes.number,
  optionalObject: PropTypes.object,
  optionalString: PropTypes.string,
  optionalSymbol: PropTypes.symbol,

//if a value of a prop is necessary
        numberType: React.PropTypes.number.isRequired
```

There is also a default type in properties via the keyword `getDefaultProps`. For example, in the same component, you can mention default types for your `text` properties:

```
static defaultProps = {
 text: 'Default Hello World'
}
```

The `defaultProps` will be used to ensure that `this.props.text` will have a value if it was not specified by the parent component.

State

In the last section, you learned about properties, which are static values that are passed into your component. State, on the other hand, is maintained and updated by the component. State is used so that a component can keep track of information in between any renders that it does. When you `setState` it updates the state object and then rerenders the component. We can think of props variables used for component initialization, whereas state is like internal data that affects the rendering of components and is considered private data.

Let's understand this concept by updating our example, creating a new component `Welcome.js` in the project folder.

```
import React, { Component } from 'react';
import PropTypes from 'prop-types';

class Welcome extends Component {
  constructor(props) {
    super(props);
    this.handleChange = this.handleChange.bind(this);
    this.state = { text: '' };
  }
  handleChange(e) {
    this.setState({ text: e.target.value });
  }
```

16

```
    render() {
      return (
        <div>
          <input
              id="text"
              onChange={this.handleChange}
              value={this.state.text}
            />
            <br />
          Welcome {this.state.text}
        </div>
      );
    }
}

Welcome.propTypes = {
  text: PropTypes.string.isRequired
};

export default Welcome;
```

Update the App.js with this:

```
import React, { Component } from 'react';
import Message from './Message';
import Welcome from './Welcome';

class App extends Component {
  render() {
    return (
      <div>
        <Welcome />
        <Message text= "Hello to React World"/>
      </div>
    );
  }
}

export default App;
```

If you run this snippet, you will see the result shown in Figure 1-8 in your browser.

Figure 1-8. *Resulting message using state*

Now when you add some name in the text box, it will automatically reflect in label, as shown in Figure 1-9.

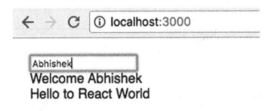

Figure 1-9. *Autopopulating the label*

Let's look at the code. In the same component, you initialized the state in constructor, in which you set up the initial state of the message and also bind the handleChange function we have created:

```
constructor(props) {
    super(props);
    this.handleChange = this.handleChange.bind(this);
    this.state = { text: '' };
}
```

Like any other language, JavaScript class has constructors, a function that will get called whenever a new object is created. It's important to call a super if we want to update the constructors. Calling this function will call the constructor of our parent class and allows it to initialize itself.

Note   The constructor is only the place where you can change or set the state by directly overwriting the `this.state` fields. In all other instances you have to use `this.setState`.

Next, unlike the last example, you access this state using `this.state.text`, which prints the initial text of the message state:

```
{this.state.text}
```

Now, display a text box above your message statement. As you type in the text box, the message gets updated in real time using the concept of state:

```
<input
      id="text"
      onChange={this.handleChange}
      value={this.state.text}
   />
```

Let's see what you added to your component. First, you introduced a function named handleChange:

```
handleChange(e) {
  this.setState({ text: e.target.value });
}
```

This new function, handleChange, takes an event called (e) and updates the value text state.

The input box has an onChange event that calls your custom method handleChange whenever the state gets updated. As you type in the text box, your printed message gets updated instantaneously.

Summary

This chapter provided a quick tour of React. Before you begin with the next chapter, let's recap what you have learned so far. We introduced the React library and the reasons behind its invention. Then you learned how to install and set up React. You studied the fundamentals of this technology, such as VDOM, one-way data flow, and JSX. You also got an introduction to components, and took a closer look at components, understanding how to use states and props with components.

Now that you are equipped to code and work in the React ecosystem, the your journey begins in the next chapter as we start working with React Native.

CHAPTER 2

The Simplest Program: Hello World with React Native

Big things have small beginnings.

—Prometheus

In the last chapter, you got a good overview of the React ecosystem. Now it's time to get your hands dirty with React Native. In this chapter, you will set up your development environment by installing the prerequisites and then you will create your first React Native application.

The best way to learn is through practical examples. We continue this theme throughout the book, as you will follow simple examples to learn React Native by programming yourself to understand the key concepts.

This chapter explores the following topics:

- An introduction to React Native

- The essentials of React Native

- The installation of React Native

- Your first application

- The anatomy of a React Native application

- How to debug your application

© Akshat Paul and Abhishek Nalwaya 2019
A. Paul and A. Nalwaya, *React Native for Mobile Development*, https://doi.org/10.1007/978-1-4842-4454-8_2

Note   You might face a situation where different projects work on different Node versions. Therefore, it's recommended you install Node Version Manager (NVM) to help keep multiple node versions that can be switched between projects.

What Is React Native?

React Native is an open source platform for developing native mobile applications; it was developed largely by a team at Facebook. The cool part of working with React Native is that your program uses standard web technologies like JavaScript (JSX), CSS, and HTML, yet your application is fully native. In other words, your application is fast and smooth, and it is equivalent to any native application built using traditional iOS technologies like Objective-C and Swift. However, React Native does not compromise in terms of performance and overall experience, like popular hybrid frameworks that use web technologies to build iOS apps.

React Native aims to bring the power of React, which was explained in Chapter 1, to mobile development. In the words of the React team, "Learn once, write anywhere." Working with React and React Native, you will see how many of your components built for the Web using React can be easily ported to your React Native iOS apps with little or no modification. React Native introduces a highly functional approach to constructing UIs that is very different from the traditional iOS development approach.

Although React Native was built by Facebook developers, it's an open source project. The code is available at `https://github.com/facebook/react-native`.

Installation

Let's do a quick, one-time setup of React Native. React Native is an assortment of JavaScript and Swift code, so you need tools that create, run, and debug your native application written in JavaScript. Let's go one by one.

Installing Node and npm

Node.js is an open source platform built on Chrome's JavaScript runtime; it offers a way to easily build fast, scalable programs. Node.js allows you to run JavaScript in terminal, and helps create modules. If you are using nvm, which is the suggested way of using node type:

```
> nvm install node
```

If you don't want to use nvm, you can also install Node.js by running the following command in terminal:

```
>brew install node.
```

Homebrew is the package manager for Mac. You can also download the Node installer from https://nodejs.org and install it manually if you are using another operating system. For Windows operating systems you can visit https://nodejs.org and install Node using a wizard.

npm is also installed along with node, which is a package manager for Node.js. If you're from the iOS world, it's similar to CocoaPods.

Check your Node installation by running the following command in terminal:

```
>> node -v
v10.8.0

>> npm -v
6.2.0
```

Installing the React Native Package

To use React Native, starting your project from scratch using create-reactive-app by Facebook is the best way to start. It is an npm module:

```
npm install -g create-react-native-app
```

Updating React Native

Both React Native and iOS are fast-moving frameworks. It is recommended that you update them every time a new release is available. Upgrading React Native is simple. First install module react-native-git-upgrade:

```
$ npm install -g react-native-git-upgrade
```

Next, run the following command to start the process of upgrading to the latest version:

```
$ react-native-git-upgrade
```

For more information on React Native upgrades, you can refer to the Facebook official documentation at `https://facebook.github.io/react-native/docs/upgrading`.

Note   You should only need to update the global installation of `create-react-native-app` very rarely, and ideally never.

Your First App

Now that you are all charged up about React Native and have your system set up, it's time to create your first application. To keep things simple, in the beginning just follow along. Sometimes you might feel disconnected by monotonously typing in the code, but following along is enough for now. Remember that mimicry is a powerful form of learning; it's how we learned most of our skills, such as talking, reading, and writing, and it's how you will learn to program with React Native. As you proceed, this method will help you understand thoroughly why you authored certain pieces of code.

Throughout the book, you will create one application and take it from just Hello World to a full-blown, distribution-level application, except in a few places, where we need to digress to explore a concept independently. Before you set it up, then, let's talk about the problem you plan to solve. The app you will create during the course of this book plans to solve a few housing problems; it will be a very primitive version of any popular property search application. Let's call it HouseShare. It will have some rudimentary features like listings, creating an entry, geolocating a property, and a few more. As you move along, you will see how various React Native features fit with your application.

That's quite a lot, but in this chapter you just create the basic structure for your project using React Native and some Hello World code.

Creating a Basic Skeleton

Fire up your terminal and type in the following command:

```
create-react-native-app HouseShare
```

...

...

...

Success! Created HouseShare at /Users/abhisheknalwaya/Documents/book/ HouseShareInside that directory, you can run several commands:

```
yarn start
```

Starts the development server so you can open your React Native app in the Expo application on your phone.

```
yarn run ios
  (Mac only, requires Xcode)
```

Starts the development server and loads your app in an iOS simulator.

```
yarn run android
  (Requires Android build tools)
```

Starts the development server and loads your app on a connected Android device or emulator.

```
yarn test
```

Starts the test runner.

```
yarn run eject
```

Removes this tool and copies build dependencies, configuration files, and scripts into the app directory. If you do this, you can't go back!

We suggest that you begin by typing this:

```
cd HouseShare
yarn start
```

Happy hacking!

So far we have used Expo a few times, so what is Expo? Expo is an open source tool chain that is built around React Native to help build iOS and Android apps. Expo is the fastest way to kickstart your React Native development. Because it comes out of the box with React Native, you don't need to perform any additional setup on your machine. The only extra thing you need to do is to install the Expo application from the Apple App Store for iOS and the Google Play Store for Android. Using this app, you will be able to test and interact with the application you are building during the development stages.

This code uses the CLI tool to construct a React Native project that is ready to build and run as is. This command creates the basic folder structure for your React Native iOS project.

```
> cd HouseShare
> yarn start
```

You should see output similar to Figure 2-1.

This will start a development server for us and print a QR code in your terminal.

```
→  HouseShare yarn start
yarn run v1.3.2
$ react-native-scripts start
10:51:52 AM: Starting packager...
Packager started!
```

```
Your app is now running at URL: exp://192.168.1.6:19000

View your app with live reloading:

   Android device:
      -> Point the Expo app to the QR code above.
         (You'll find the QR scanner on the Projects tab of the app.)
   iOS device:
      -> Press s to email/text the app URL to your phone.
   Emulator:
      -> Press a (Android) or i (iOS) to start an emulator.

Your phone will need to be on the same local network as this computer.
For links to install the Expo app, please visit https://expo.io.

Logs from serving your app will appear here. Press Ctrl+C at any time to stop.

 › Press a to open Android device or emulator, or i to open iOS emulator.
 › Press s to send the app URL to your phone number or email address
 › Press q to display QR code.
 › Press r to restart packager, or R to restart packager and clear cache.
 › Press d to toggle development mode. (current mode: development)
```

Figure 2-1. *Terminal output when we build a React Native application*

To use this QR code, download the Expo app (`https://expo.io/`) for iOS or Android on your device.

If you are using Android, just scan the QR code in your terminal from the Expo app and your app we automatically load. If you are using iOS, select "s" in your terminal, as shown in Figure 2-2.

Now open the e-mail, shown in Figure 2-3:

```
Please enter your phone number or email address (press ESC to cancel)
[[default: nalwayaabhishek@gmail.com]>
12:46:20 PM: Sending exp://192.168.1.6:19000 to nalwayaabhishek@gmail.com...
12:46:21 PM: Sent link successfully.

 › Press a to open Android device or emulator, or i to open iOS emulator.
 › Press s to send the app URL to your phone number or email address
 › Press q to display QR code.
 › Press r to restart packager, or R to restart packager and clear cache.
 › Press d to toggle development mode. (current mode: development)
```

Figure 2-2. *Press the s key if you are using iOS*

Figure 2-3. *Expo link received in e-mail*

Note   Your mobile device needs to be connected to the same wireless network as your computer. Otherwise you will not able to open the app.

If the Expo app is already installed on your device and you click the link it will automatically run the React Native app in the Expo app, as shown in Figure 2-4.

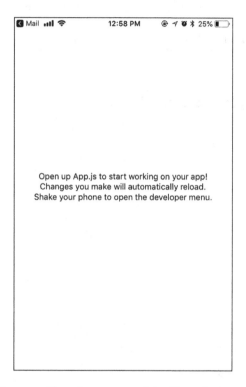

Figure 2-4. *React Native application opened in Expo app*

That was really quick and easy. Without installing the iOS and Android software development kit (SDK), we can run the app on our device using Expo.

Thanks to a single command, the basic structure of your project is in place and your application is loaded in the device. Also note that the terminal always needs to be open. This is the Node package manager for React Native. If you kill this, the app will stop working.

Terminal is opened to start the React Native Packager and a server to handle the preceding request. The React Native Packager is responsible for reading and building the JSX (you'll look at this later) and JavaScript code.

Set up your project in any editor you prefer. React Native does not force you to use nor does it have a preference for any specific editor, so you can continue to use your favorites.

Now let's update some code in our application. Add the following code in App.js:

```
import React from 'react';
import { StyleSheet, Text, View } from 'react-native';

export default class App extends React.Component {
  render() {
    return (
      <View style={styles.container}>
        <Text>
          Hello World
        </Text>
      </View>
    );
  }
}

const styles = StyleSheet.create({
  container: {
    flex: 1,
    backgroundColor: '#fff',
    alignItems: 'center',
    justifyContent: 'center',
  },
});
```

Just save the file, and then check the Expo app on your device. It automatically reloads the page and shows you the screen shown in Figure 2-5.

Figure 2-5. *Updated text component appears on the screen on save*

That was quick! In a fraction of a second you can see the changes you applied. You don't need to compile the code and restart the simulator for React Native changes. If you have done any native iOS app development before, pressing Refresh to see the changes might seem like a miracle.

Now, let's understand the code. At the top of the file are the following lines:

```
import React from 'react';
import { StyleSheet, Text, View } from 'react-native';
```

This loads the React module and assigns it to a React variable that can be used in your code. React Native uses the same module-loading technology as Node.js; this is roughly equivalent to linking and importing libraries in Swift.

You are assigning multiple object properties to a single variable; this is called destructuring the assignment. This cool feature is in there in versions of JavaScript after ES6. Although it is optional, it's very beneficial; otherwise, every time you use a component in your code, you would have to use a fully qualified name for it, such as React.Stylesheet, and so on. This saves quite a bit of time.

Next, you create a view:

```
export default class App extends React.Component {
  render() {
    return (
      <View style={styles.container}>
        <Text>
          Hello World
        </Text>
      </View>
    );
  }
}
```

React basic building blocks are called components. You can use the React.Component method to create custom component classes. This class has just one function, render(), which is responsible for what is shown on the screen. You use JavaScript syntax extensions (JSX) for rendering the UI. JSX is a JavaScript syntax extension that looks similar to XML.

Now you define the styling of your app. Here you will use Flexbox; it is similar to what CSS is to HTML. For now, you can type this code. We explain styling in the next chapter.

```
const styles = StyleSheet.create({
  container: {
    flex: 1,
    backgroundColor: '#fff',
    alignItems: 'center',
    justifyContent: 'center',
  },
});
```

You can see that this styling is very similar to CSS; you can define font size, alignment, and so on.

Prerequisites for Running App on a Simulator

Using the Expo iOS or Android application to test your app, there is a downside: You can't always carry your devices for testing your application. For such purpose there are simulators provided by both iOS and Android to be set up on your development machine. The following are few prerequisites to set them up.

iOS

- iOS apps can be developed only on an Apple Mac with OSX installed. You need OSX version 11 or above.

- You need Xcode 9 or above, which includes the iOS SDK and simulators. React Native only supports iOS7 or above. Xcode can be downloaded from the Apple App Store.

- It's helpful if you are enrolled in the Apple iOS Developer Program. If you're not in the iOS Developer Program, you won't be able to do the following:

    - Test applications on actual devices.

    - Access beta OS releases.

    - Test flight for beta testing.

    - Submit your app to the App Store.

Android

- React Native requires a recent version of the Java SE Development Kit (JDK).

- Download and install Android Studio. Choose a Custom setup when prompted to select an installation type. Make sure the check boxes next to all of the following are selected:

    - Android SDK

    - Android SDK Platform

    - Performance (Intel $^{®}$ HAXM)

    - Android Virtual Device

- Install Android Virtual Devices (AVDs) by opening the AVD Manager from within Android Studio. You can also use genymotion.

Running the App on a Simulator

Now let's go back to our application and start the app (see Figure 2-6):

```
yarn start
```

Figure 2-6. *Running demo application on simulator*

This will install Expo client on the emulator and run your React Native app. You can also use commands like `yarn ios` or `yarn android` to start the simulator with the app installed in it rather than loading the app inside the Expo simulator app.

It's Not a UIWebView

You are using web technologies, but your app does not have a web component; it has a native component. Open Debug ➤ View Debugging ➤ Capture View Hierarchy (see Figure 2-7).

Figure 2-7. *Using the Native component*

As you traverse through the tree of UIWindow, you'll see that there is no UIWebView in the code, and "Hello World !!" is the call of RCTText, as shown in Figure 2-8.

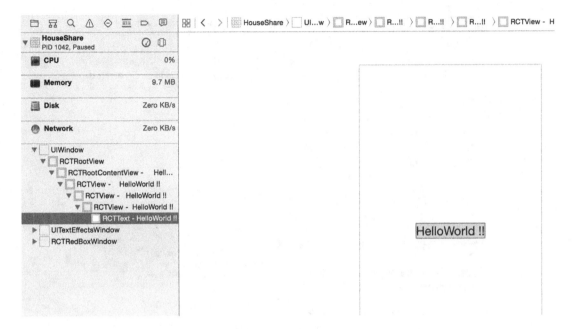

Figure 2-8. *"Hello World !!" is the call of RCTText*

Enabling Live Reload

Another cool feature of React Native is live reload. It reloads your application view inside the iOS simulator the moment there is a change. By default it is active. To deactivate this option, you need to access the developer menu from the application opened in the iOS simulator by shaking the device and then selecting the Disable Live Reload option.

What Makes React Native Different?

Before you dive deeper into the React Native world, you must understand why there was a need for another framework to build mobile apps. We already live in a world full of frameworks and tool chains that are capable of building mobile apps. Prior to the inception of React Native, building mobile apps using web technologies was possible via two strategies:

- *WebView-based*: These frameworks use common web technologies like HTML and JavaScript and use WebView to load the application. An example is the popular framework Phonegap.

- *Native apps using web technologies*: These frameworks again use common web technologies like HTML and JavaScript (to be precise, they imitate using JavaScript and HTML) to create native apps. An example is the popular framework Titanium Appcelerator.

Apps created using these strategies have performance issues. WebView-based apps are slow because they use the DOM, and DOM manipulations are expensive, which leads to performance issues. As stated in a blog post at Flipboard (see http://engineering.flipboard.com/2015/02/mobile-web/), "You cannot build a 60fps scrolling list view with DOM." This is one of the fundamental problems with apps developed through this technique: Although development time might be quick, you end up with a sluggish experience.

The other strategy, where the framework imitates JavaScript and HTML, and converts them to native code, has other challenges. Although the final app is native in nature, there is a basic issue during this conversion from JavaScript to native: It runs on the main thread. In these apps, you interface directly with native objects all the time, which leads once again to a slow and sluggish experience.

React Native is fundamentally different from these two approaches. It runs all layouts on separate threads, and your main thread is free to update the UI, which makes the animation and UI rendering smooth, just like 100 percent pure native apps.

React Native uses the JavaScriptCore framework to run JavaScript. In iOS 7, Apple introduced a native Objective-C API for JavaScriptCore. This framework allows JavaScript and Objective-C to talk to each other. This means you can create and call JavaScript functions from Objective-C or call back into Objective-C from JavaScript. It all works like a charm.

React Native is different in one more aspect. As seen in your Hello World example, you write a component in JavaScript just like you would with React, except that instead of using an HTML div, you use tags like View and Text. In the case of an iOS application, a View is basically a UIView.

Ejecting a React Native Application

Before we get into exploring the application structure, we have to eject our application from the Expo project (see Figure 2-9). You should not eject an app from the Expo environment until it is needed. We are doing this here to understand how create-react-native works.

```
yarn eject
```

```
[→  HouseShare yarn eject
yarn run v1.3.2
$ react-native-scripts eject

We didn't find any uses of the Expo SDK in your project, so you should be fine to eject to
"Plain" React Native. (This check isn't very sophisticated, though.)

We strongly recommend that you read this document before you proceed:
    https://github.com/react-community/create-react-native-app/blob/master/EJECTING.md

Ejecting is permanent! Please be careful with your selection.

? How would you like to eject from create-react-native-app? React Native: I'd like a regular React Native project.
We have a couple of questions to ask you about how you'd like to name your app:
[? What should your app appear as on a user's home screen? HouseShare
[? What should your Android Studio and Xcode projects be called? HouseShare
Writing your selections to app.json...
Wrote to app.json, please update it manually in the future.
Scanning folders for symlinks in /Users/abhisheknalwaya/Documents/book/HouseShare/node_modules (21ms)
Generating the iOS folder.
Generating the Android folder.
Successfully copied template native code.
Babel preset changed to `babel-preset-react-native-stage-0/decorator-support`.
Updating your yarn scripts in package.json...
Your package.json is up to date!
Adding entry point...
Added new entry points!

Note that using `yarn start` will now require you to run Xcode and/or
Android Studio to build the native code for your project.
Removing node_modules...
Installing packages with yarn...
[1/4] 🔍  Resolving packages...
[2/4] 🚚  Fetching packages...
[3/4] 🔗  Linking dependencies...
warning "react-native > eslint-plugin-react-native@3.2.1" has unmet peer dependency "eslint@^3.17.0 || ^4.0.0".
[4/4] 📦  Building fresh packages...
success Saved lockfile.
success Saved 48 new dependencies.
├─ babel-jest@23.4.2
├─ babel-plugin-istanbul@4.1.6
├─ babel-plugin-jest-hoist@23.2.0
├─ babel-plugin-syntax-class-constructor-call@6.18.0
├─ babel-plugin-syntax-do-expressions@6.13.0
├─ babel-plugin-syntax-function-bind@6.13.0
├─ babel-plugin-transform-class-constructor-call@6.24.1
├─ babel-plugin-transform-do-expressions@6.22.0
├─ babel-plugin-transform-export-extensions@6.22.0
├─ babel-plugin-transform-function-bind@6.22.0
├─ babel-preset-jest@23.2.0
├─ babel-preset-react-native-stage-0@1.0.1
├─ babel-preset-react-native@1.9.2
├─ browser-resolve@1.11.3
├─ expect@23.5.0
├─ istanbul-api@1.3.1
├─ jest-changed-files@23.4.2
├─ jest-cli@23.5.0
├─ jest-config@23.5.0
├─ jest-diff@23.5.0
├─ jest-docblock@23.2.0
├─ jest-each@23.5.0
├─ jest-environment-jsdom@23.4.0
├─ jest-environment-node@23.4.0
├─ jest-haste-map@23.5.0
├─ jest-jasmine2@23.5.0
├─ jest-leak-detector@23.5.0
```

Figure 2-9. *Ejecting Expo application*

This will create two folders for iOS and Android in the repository. If you open the project HouseShare, it looks like a normal Xcode project. It has the following folder structure:

```
|ios
  |- HouseShare
  |- HouseShare.xcodeproj
  |- HouseShareTests
|android
node_modules
App.js
App.test.js
```

```
index.js
package.json
yarn.lock
```

Note   The folder structure defined here might be changed or modified as the framework evolves, but the majority of the functionality remains the same.

If you open the project in Xcode, it will have a different folder structure. The "folders" in Xcode are actually groups and are not necessarily linked to a folder like we see in Finder.

- iOS: The iOS folder has two folders and one file. As seen earlier, there is a HouseShare folder, which has all the Objective-C code, such as AppDelegate, Images.xcassets, Info.plistLaunchScreen.xib, and other files. Another folder is HouseShareTests, which is where all your test cases reside. Finally, there is your Xcode project file, HouseShare.xcodeproj, which is used to load into Xcode to build your application.

- package.json: This folder contains metadata about your app, and it will install all dependencies when you run the npm install. If you're familiar with Ruby, it's similar to a Gemfile.

- node_modules: All of the Node modules mentioned in package.json will be downloaded to this folder. This folder also contains the code for the React Native framework.

- App.js: This is the file where you begin programming your application.

- AppDelegate.m: This is the starting point of any iOS app.

- Android: React Native also supports development for Android. All your native Android code resides in this folder.

Let's open the AppDelegate.m file from HouseShare/ios/HouseShare/ AppDelegate.m:

```
#import "AppDelegate.h"
```

```objc
#import <React/RCTBundleURLProvider.h>
#import <React/RCTRootView.h>

@implementation AppDelegate

- (BOOL)application:(UIApplication *)application didFinishLaunchingWith
  Options:(NSDictionary *)launchOptions
{
  NSURL *jsCodeLocation;

  jsCodeLocation = [[RCTBundleURLProvider sharedSettings] jsBundleURLFor
                BundleRoot:@"index" fallbackResource:nil];

  RCTRootView *rootView = [[RCTRootView alloc] initWithBundleURL:jsCode
                          Location
  moduleName:@"HouseShare"
  initialProperties:nil
  launchOptions:launchOptions];
  rootView.backgroundColor = [[UIColor alloc] initWithRed:1.0f green:1.0f
                              blue:1.0f alpha:1];

  self.window = [[UIWindow alloc] initWithFrame:[UIScreen mainScreen].bounds];
  UIViewController *rootViewController = [UIViewController new];
  rootViewController.view = rootView;
  self.window.rootViewController = rootViewController;
  [self.window makeKeyAndVisible];
  return YES;
}

@end
```

RCTRootView is a Swift class provided by React Native, which is inherited from the iOS UIView Class. It takes your JavaScript code and executes it. It also loads the index bundle URL, which has your code written in App.js and also a program added by the React Native framework.

Note   After ejection, you need to use Xcode to run the iOS app and Android Studio to run the Android app.

To start, run `yarn start` on terminal, as shown in Figure 2-10.

```
[→ HouseShare yarn start
yarn run v1.3.2
$ react-native start
Scanning folders for symlinks in /Users/abhisheknalwaya/Documents/book/HouseShare/node_modules (23ms)

    Running Metro Bundler on port 8081.

    Keep Metro running while developing on any JS projects. Feel free to
    close this tab and run your own Metro instance if you prefer.

    https://github.com/facebook/react-native


Looking for JS files in
    /Users/abhisheknalwaya/Documents/book/HouseShare

Metro Bundler ready.

Loading dependency graph, done.
```

Figure 2-10. *Starting the application without Expo*

Now open `HouseShare.xcodeproj`. This Xcode project file will open your project in Xcode. Next, let's load your application in the iOS simulator. To build your application and load it in the simulator, simply click the Run button at the top left (or execute Command + R), as shown in Figure 2-11. This will compile, build, and fire up your project in the iOS simulator

Figure 2-11. *Building the application using Xcode*

This will open the simulator and you can see the app running.

Debugging

Debugging with React Native is in line with how we debug web apps; in short, it's really simple. To access debugging options, share the simulator by selecting Share Gesture from the Hardware menu. This will open a menu that provides several debugging options, as shown in Figure 2-12.

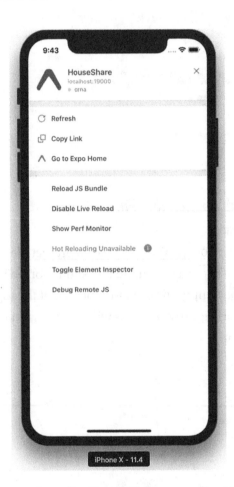

Figure 2-12. *Debugging options for React Native applications*

You must disable this menu for the final build because your end user should not see these options. To disable it, open the project in Xcode and select Product ➤ Scheme ➤ Edit Scheme (or press Command + <). Then select Run from the menu on the left and change the Build Configuration to Release.

Let's review each of the options shown in Figure 2-12.

Reload

The Reload option refreshes the screen in the simulator with the latest React Native code without compiling the project again. This can be done in two ways: selecting the Reload option from the menu or pressing Command + R. This will reload all the changes made in the JavaScript code.

Any changes made in your Swift or Objective-C files will not be reflected because these changes require recompilation. Also, if you add any assets like images, the app needs to be restarted.

Debugging in Chrome

This is one of the best and most frequently used options for debugging your JavaScript code written in React Native. As with web apps, you can debug your React Native application in Chrome. When you click Debug in Chrome, it opens `http://localhost:8081/debugger-ui` in Chrome (Figure 2-13).

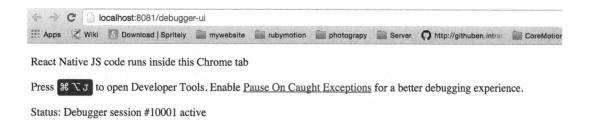

Figure 2-13. *Debugging in Chrome*

Install the React Developer Tools, which is a Chrome extension for debugging both your React application and React Native code. It allows you to inspect the React Native component hierarchies in the Chrome Developer Tools. To install it, please visit the Chrome webstore or go to `https://chrome.google.com/webstore/detail/react-developer-tools/fmkadmapgofadopljbjfkapdkoienihi?hl=en`.

Once the extension is installed, press Command + Option + J or select View ➤ Developer ➤ Developer Tools in your Chrome browser to access the Developer Tools console.

You will see a new tab called React in your Chrome DevTools. This shows you the root React components that have been rendered on the page, as well as the subcomponents that they ended up rendering. You can also see props, state, components, and event listeners, as shown in Figure 2-14.

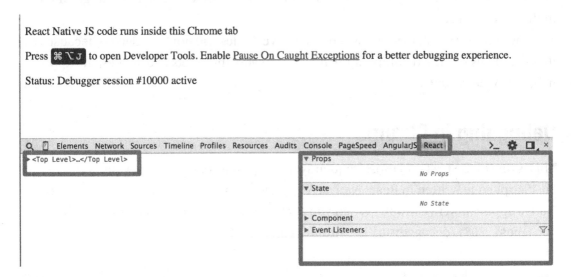

Figure 2-14. *Debugging in Chrome DevTools*

Look at Figure 2-15 and you can see a similar hierarchy to your Xcode: Hello World is wrapped in RCTText and that is in turn wrapped in RCTview.

```
  ▼ <RCTView style="75">
    ▼ <Unknown style="76">
      ▼ <RCTText style="76" accessible="true" isHighlighted="false">
          "HelloWorld !!"
      </RCTText>
    </Unknown>
  </RCTView>
```

Figure 2-15. *Debugging the app with the React tab in Chrome DevTools*

Debugging in Safari

If you do not have Chrome, you can also use Safari for debugging, but Chrome is preferred for debugging React Native apps.

Showing Performance Monitor

Many applications use a lot of animations and graphics. The smoothness of these animations for your application is defined in frames per second (FPS); this is used extensively in gaming apps. When you select Show FPS Monitor from the menu, it shows a few properties for your app in the simulator (see Figure 2-16). Although you might not find much use for these properties in your Hello World app, they are great for animation-intensive apps to prevent them lethargic performance, which can create a bumpy user experience.

Figure 2-16. *Additional properties in the simulator*

The Inspect Element

You can also inspect a React Native element from the simulator, somewhat similar to how you inspect an element in a browser, although you can't currently change live values of properties as you can in a browser. For now, you can see your stylesheet properties for any object. Click the HelloReact!! text (Figure 2-17) and it will open the details of that element.

Figure 2-17. *Click the text to see element details*

The details of that element are shown in Figure 2-18 at the bottom left.

Figure 2-18. *Font details*

You can see that the font size for Hello World is 25 and it is center aligned.

Summary

In this chapter, you were introduced to React Native. You learned how to set up the React Native development environment and you wrote your first application. You also learned about Expo and the folder structure of React Native applications and how to debug. You are now all set to explore creating a UI with React Native for your iOS application.

Chapter 3 introduces about Flux and Redux, a pair of very important design patterns that are commonly used with React Native applications.

CHAPTER 3

Solving Problems Differently with Flux and Redux

Simplicity is prerequisite for reliability.

—Djikstra

Flux is an application architecture introduced by Facebook for building client-side applications. It complements the React paradigm of composable view components by using a unidirectional data flow. It's more of a pattern than a framework, and one can start using Flux immediately without an excess load of code. Redux is a predictable state container for JavaScript applications, which means it helps us to write applications that behave consistently in different environments: client, server, or native. It also makes your applications easy to debug and test.

Before we delve into its details, it is important to know one of the most popular, commonly used MVC patterns. We can then learn about what challenges we face with MVC and how Flux and Redux can solve these challenges.

This chapter covers the following topics:

- MVC pattern

- MVC problem

- Flux

- Flux deep dive

- Redux

© Akshat Paul and Abhishek Nalwaya 2019   49
A. Paul and A. Nalwaya, *React Native for Mobile Development*, https://doi.org/10.1007/978-1-4842-4454-8_3

- Redux core concepts

- Redux with React Native

- Benefits of using Redux

MVC Pattern

Historically, an MVC pattern separates code into three distinct parts: model, view, and controller. The main purpose of this pattern is to isolate representation of information from user interaction. Let's describe each of these parts individually.

- *Model:* This element manages the behavior and data of an application.

- *View:* This is the representation layer of the model in the UI.

- *Controller:* This element takes user input and makes necessary manipulations to the model, which causes the view layer to get updated.

MVC is legendary and it's an amazing way to structure your code. Things get a bit ugly, though, when your source code begins to grow and get complex. Although MVC is a very popular pattern to design applications, it comes with its own set of problems. Figure 3-1 shows how MVC works.

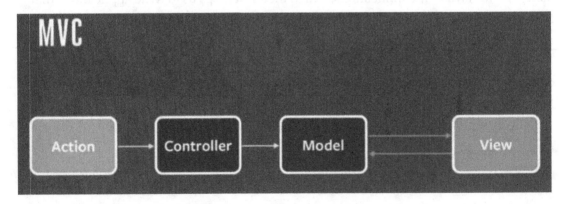

Figure 3-1. *Simple MVC pattern*

Figure 3-1 shows the simplest implementation of MVC, and this works pretty well with small applications. As your application grows, though, so does the demand for new features, and there should be room to accommodate more models and views. Let's look at what happens when our model and view increase in an actual application (Figure 3-2).

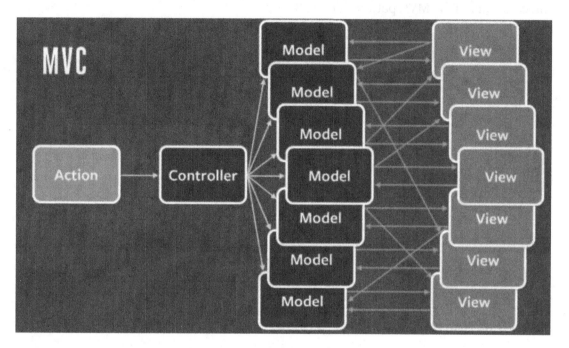

Figure 3-2. *MVC pattern for a large application*

Wow! That is an explosion of arrows. Welcome to the real world where many models and views interact with each other. A controller triggers another model and this goes on like spaghetti, which often ends up in an infinite loop. The worst part is that it's really difficult to debug code in such a situation, eventually making the system fragile. Well, Facebook faced a similar problem with this pattern and solved it with a new pattern called Flux.

Flux

Flux abjures MVC in favor of a unidirectional data flow. Flux works well because the single directional data flow makes it easy to understand and modify an application as it grows and becomes more complex. Earlier we found that two-way data bindings lead to cascading updates, where change in one data model leads to an update in another data model, making it very difficult to predict what would change as the result of a single user interaction.

Flux applications have three major parts: the dispatcher, the store, and the view (where we use React components). These should not be compared with the model, view, and controller of the MVC pattern (Figure 3-3).

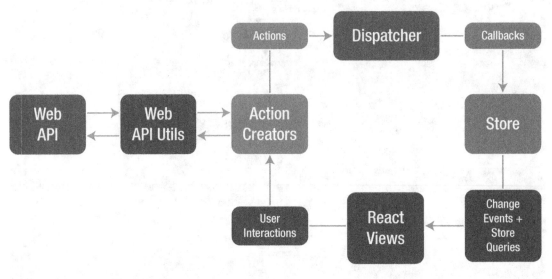

Figure 3-3. *React App data flow*

Although controllers do exist in a Flux application, these are controller views, where views are found at the top of the hierarchy that retrieve data from the stores and forward these data to their children.

If we look at the Flux architecture, the most important part is the dispatcher, which is a singleton that directs the flow of data and ensures that updates do not cascade (Figure 3-4).

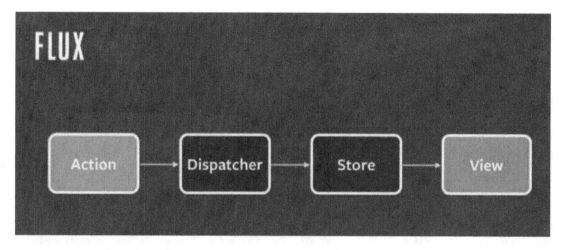

Figure 3-4. *Flux data flow*

As an application grows, eventually the dispatcher becomes more vital, as it is responsible for managing dependencies between stores by invoking the registered callbacks in a specific order.

When a user interacts with a React view, the view sends an action (usually represented as a JavaScript object with some fields) through the dispatcher, which notifies the various stores that hold the application's data and business logic. When the stores change state, they notify the views that something has updated. This works especially well with React's declarative model, which allows the stores to send updates without specifying how to transition views between states.

The following are some of the key benefits of using Flux:

- It improves data consistency.

- It is easier to pinpoint the bugs.

- You can perform more meaningful unit tests. Because all the states of a module are there in the same place, we can test a module independently.

- It includes predictable code.

With predictable code, great things follow, as shown in Figure 3-5.

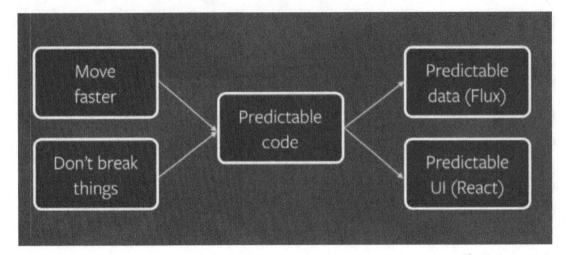

Figure 3-5. Predictable code

Success of Flux

One of Facebook's most popular features was its chat functionality. However, it was extremely buggy and had a high rate of negative user feedback. The new chat system that Facebook implemented is using a Flux pattern that provides a seamless experience. You can have look at example chat code in a Facebook React example at `https://github.com/facebook/flux/tree/master/examples`.

Flux Deep Dive

As we now know what Flux is, let's look into and understand the concepts like dispatcher, store, and action

The Dispatcher

The dispatcher is the central hub that manages all data flow in a Flux application. It is essentially a registry of callbacks into the stores and has no real intelligence of its own; in essence, it is a simple mechanism for distributing the actions to the stores. Each store registers itself and provides a callback. When an action creator provides the dispatcher with a new action, all stores in the application receive the action via the callbacks in the registry. Dispatcher also acts like a traffic controller. If it gets an action even when the data layer is still processing, it makes sure to run the action. With the dispatcher, you know where your action starts and what changes it makes to the data layer. There are cascading effects that build up in between. You are indeed in full control of your system.

The Need for Dispatcher [dispatch() and waitFor()]

As an application grows, dependencies across different stores also increase. Imagine, for example, we have a situation where Store A needs Store B to update itself first, so that it can itself know how to update, too. We need the dispatcher to be able to invoke the callback for Store B and finish that callback before moving forward with Store A. To assert this dependence, a store needs to communicate with the dispatcher to first complete the action to update Store B. The dispatcher provides this functionality through the waitFor() method.

The dispatch() method provides a simple, synchronous iteration through the callbacks, invoking each in turn. When waitFor() is encountered within one of the callbacks, execution of that callback stops and waitFor() provides us with a new iteration cycle over the dependencies. After the entire set of dependencies has been fulfilled, the original callback then continues to execute.

Further, the waitFor() method can be used in different ways for different actions, within the same store's callback. In one case, Store A might need to wait for Store B. In another case, though, it might need to wait for Store C. Using waitFor() within the code block that is specific to an action allows us to have fine-grained control of these dependencies.

Problems arise, however, if we have circular dependencies; that is, if Store A needs to wait for Store B, and Store B needs to wait for Store A. This could wind up in an endless loop. The dispatcher now available in the Flux repo protects against this by throwing an informative error to alert the developer that this problem has occurred. The developer can then create a third store and resolve the circular dependency.

Stores

Stores contain the application state and logic. Their role is somewhat similar to a model in a traditional MVC, but they manage the state of many objects—they do not represent a single record of data like ORM (Object Relational Mapping) models do. More than simply managing a collection of ORM-style objects, stores manage the application state for a particular domain within the application.

As mentioned earlier, a store registers itself with the dispatcher and provides it with a callback. This callback receives the action as a parameter. Within the store's registered callback, a switch statement based on the action's type is used to interpret the action and to provide the proper hooks into the store's internal methods. This allows an action to result in an update to the state of the store via the dispatcher. After the stores are updated, they broadcast an event declaring that their state has changed, so the views can query the new state and update themselves.

Actions

When new data enter the system, whether through a person interacting with the application or through a web API call, those data are packaged into an action—an object literal containing the new fields of data and a specific action type. We often create a library of helper methods called action creators that not only create the action object, but also pass the action to the dispatcher.

Different actions are identified by a type attribute. When all of the stores receive the action, they typically use this attribute to determine if and how they should respond to it. In a Flux application, both stores and views control themselves; external objects do not act on them. Actions flow into the stores through the callbacks they define and register, not through setter methods.

Letting the stores update themselves eliminates many entanglements typically found in MVC applications, where ascading updates between models can lead to unstable state and make accurate testing very difficult. The objects within a Flux application are highly decoupled, and adhere very strongly to the Law of Demeter, the principle that each object within a system should know as little as possible about the other objects in the system. This results in software that is more maintainable, adaptable, testable, and easier for new engineering team members to understand.

Redux

Now that we have read about Flux, next we discuss another pattern called Redux. Redux can be considered a predecessor to the Flux architecture, and it is also inspired by the functional programming language Elm. Redux was created by Dan Abramov in mid-2015. During that time, the React world was going through major changes and new things were coming every other day. No one, though, could imagine that a small library of just 2 KB would create such a tectonic shift in the way we interact with and create React applications.

Redux was built on top of functional programming concepts. Functional programming by design allows us to write clean and modular code that is easier to test, debug, and maintain. With functional programming, code is in the form of small functions that are isolated in scope and logic, thus making the code reusable. Because small pieces of code are isolated in nature, there is hardly any coupling and these tiny functions can be used as modules in an app. In functional JavaScript you will see pure functions, anonymous functions, and higher order functions used very often. Redux uses pure functions a lot, so a good understanding of this concept is important.

Pure functions return a value based on arguments passed to them. They do not modify or mutate existing objects, but they return new ones. These functions do not depend on the state from which they are called, but they return only one and the same result for any provided argument. That's why they are very predictable. Because pure functions do not modify any value, they don't have any observable side effects. Redux uses something called reducers, which are pure functions. We will learn in detail about reducers and other Redux code concepts in the next section.

Redux Core Concepts

Redux has three core pillars: action, store, and reducers (Figure 3-6). These words might sound complicated, but they are actually very simple.

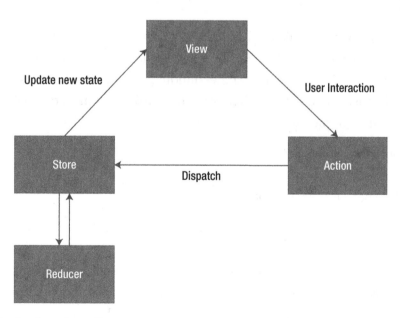

Figure 3-6. *Redux data flow*

Action

Actions are events that send data from the application (user interactions, API calls, form submissions, etc.) to the store. The store always gets the information from actions. Internal actions are simple JavaScript objects that have a type property (usually constant), describing the type of action and payload of information being sent to the store. To send them to the store we use `store.dispatch()`.

Action creators, as the name suggests, are the functions that create actions. It is easy to conflate the terms *action* and *action creator,* so do your best to use the proper term. To call these action creator functions anywhere in the app we use dispatch. As mentioned earlier, the `dispatch()` function can be accessed directly from the store as `store.dispatch()`, but more likely you'll access it using a helper like react-redux's `connect()` method. You can use `bindActionCreators()` to automatically bind many action creators to a `dispatch()` function.

Note   Action creators can also be asynchronous and have side effects. This is an advanced topic, so we don't need to go in-depth right now.

Reducer

Reducers specify how the application's state changes in response to actions sent to the store. Remember that actions only describe what has happened, but do not tell anything about state change in the application. Understanding how reducers work is important in an application using Redux because they are responsible for most of the work. Let's describe this with a simple example.

```
function appAuth(state, action) {
    return Object .assign({}, state, {
        authType: action.payload
    });
}
```

This is a very simple reducer that takes the current state and an action as arguments and then returns the next state. In the case of complex applications, we will be using the `combineReducers()` utility that is provided by Redux. It combines all the reducers of the app into a single index reducer. Every reducer is responsible for its own part of the app's state, and the state parameter is different for every reducer. The `combineReducers()` utility makes the file structure much easier to maintain.

Store

Thus far we have learned that actions represent what happened and the reducers update the state according to those actions. The store is the object that brings them all together. The store holds the application state and provides a few helper methods to access the state, dispatch actions, and register listeners. The entire state is represented by a single store. Any action returns a new state via reducers. The following are few helper methods:

- `getState()`: Allows access to state.

- `dispatch(action)`: Allows state to be updated.

- `subscribe(listener)`: Registers listeners.

- `replaceReducer(nextReducer)`: Replaces the reducer currently used by the store to calculate the state.

Redux with React Native

To understand how Redux works with React Native, let's create a simple Todo application in React Native including how Redux makes things simple for us. To proceed, use the source code available for this chapter. Inside the project directory, run `yarn install` to install two new packages.

```
redux
react-redux
```

The Redux module is required so that you can use Redux with your application. React-redux is going to help you connect your React native app to Redux once you have both of these installed. Figure 3-7 shows our application folder structure.

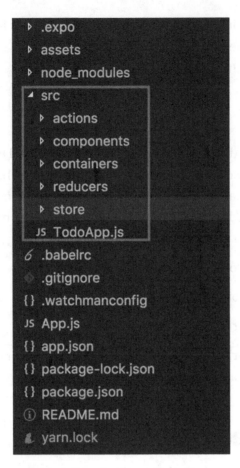

Figure 3-7. *List of project folder structure*

You would have to create all these folders: components, containers, reducers, store, and a `TodoApp.js` file. Within these folders we would have more JavaScript files reside inside our action, stores, reducers, and components. This way our code stays modularized and the logic remains isolated. Here, the Redux part is managed under the action, reducer, and the store folder, but we would need components that will use them.

Hence, we have two folders here: `components`, which consists of plain dumb components, which are the presentational components of the app having no idea that Redux exists or not in the app. Second, we have smart components that interact with Redux, and they reside in the `containers` folder.

First, let's create a store. Inside the store folder create an index.js file and paste the following code:

```
import { createStore } from 'redux'
import rootReducer from '../reducers'

export default store = createStore(rootReducer)
```

Here, we have imported something called createStore from redux. Here we are combining all our reducers with rootReducer and exporting the same. Soon you will see how we have created two reducers that we plan to use with our store using rootReducer.

Next, this store is imported into the application by adding the following code in our App.js.

```
import store from './src/store'
import { Provider } from 'react-redux'
export default class App extends React.Component {
  render() {
    return (
      <Provider store={store}>
        <TodoApp />
      </Provider>
    );
  }
}
```

Here, we have imported our store and also used something called Provider from react-redux. Once we pass our Provider and store within that, it can be accessed anywhere in TodoApp no matter how many levels deep it is. Great! With this our store is set up.

Although our store is setup, we require some UI components. If you look at the containers folder, we have an addTodo component, which is a simple TextInput that will be used to create a new todo. Therefore, on this text input field there will be some action that will trigger it to create a new todo.

Before we create our action and reducer, we must think about what states we can have in this application. As per our design, there should be two states: one Todo and one for visibility. Therefore, in the reducers folder, you will find two files: one for the todo reducer and other for the visibilityFilter reducer.

```
const visibilityFilter = (state = "SHOW_ALL", action) => {
    return state
}
```

Here the visibility filter reducer takes the state SHOW_ALL and based on the action, it gives the expected outcome and returns the state. In this case, it is responsible to show all the todo records. Next, let's look at the todo reducer:

```
const todos = (state = [], action) => {
    switch (action.type) {
        case 'ADD_TODO':
            return [
                ...state, {
                    id: action.id,
                    text: action.text,
                    completed: false
                }
            ]

        case 'TOGGLE_TODO':
            return state.map(todo =>
                (todo.id === action.id)
                    ? { ...todo, completed: !todo.completed } :
                    todo)
        default:
            return state
    }
}

export default todos
```

Here we have two actions—ADD_TODO and TOGGLE_TODO—that are responsible for adding a new record in the list and marking a record complete using their respective actions. We are able to determine the type of actions using action.type.

At this point, both the reducers are independent, so we need a way to combine them, which you can find in the third file in the reducers folder, index.js. Let's look at the code inside reducers/index.js.

```
import { combineReducers } from 'redux'
import todos from './todos'
import visibilityFilter from './visibilityFilter'

export default combineReducers({
    todos,
    visibilityFilter
})
```

Here we are using something called `CombineReducers` from redux. This helps is keep the logical part separate but use it such in a way that we have only one reducer.

Working with the Components

Now that we have seen our reducers, let's see how all this so far works with our components. Open the `containers/AddTodo.js` file.

```
import { connect } from 'react-redux '
import { addTodo } from '../actions'

class AddTodo extends Component {

    state = {
        text: ' '
    }

    addTodo = (text) => {
        // redux store
        this.props.dispatch(addTodo(text))
        this.setState({ text: '' })
    }

    render() {
        return (
            <View style={{ flexDirection: 'row', marginHorizontal: 20 }}>
                <TextInput
                    onChangeText={(text) => this.setState({ text })}
                    value={this.state.text}
```

```
                    placeholder="E.g. Create New Video"
                    style={{ borderWidth: 1, borderColor: '#f2f2e1',
                    backgroundColor: '#eaeaea', height: 50, flex: 1,
                    padding: 5 }}
                />
                <TouchableOpacity onPress={() => this.addTodo(this.state.
                text)}>
                    <View style={{ height: 50, backgroundColor: '#eaeaea',
                    alignItems: 'center', justifyContent: 'center' }}>
                        <Ionicons name="md-add" size={30} style={{ color:
                        '#de9595', padding: 10 }} />
                    </View>
                </TouchableOpacity>
            </View>
        );
    }
}
export default connect()(AddTodo);
```

Here, we first have to set up the initial local state:

```
state = {
    text: ''
 }
```

This is just an empty string for the text input to stay empty. Next, we have to update the text from text input when a user types. This is done using onChangeText where the state is updated with the text entered by the user.

```
onChangeText={(text) => this.setState({ text })}
                value={this.state.text}
```

Once the user submits the todo it must be updated to our store. For this, we use a helper method, connect, from react-redux.

```
import { connect } from 'react-redux'
```

In addition, the `connect` helper method should be passed with the component that is going to get connected to the Redux store. In this case, use `AddTodo`:

```
export default connect()(AddTodo);
```

We also have to import the action we plan to use; in this case, it is `addTodo`:

```
import { addTodo } from '../actions'
```

Great! Now that we have connected our store to the component, let's trigger it `onPress` to add the `todo` in a list:

```
<TouchableOpacity onPress={() => this.addTodo(this.state.text)}>
```

Because this component is connected to the Redux store, we can dispatch the action to the respective store:

```
addTodo = (text) => {
     this.props.dispatch(addTodo(text))
     this.setState({ text: '' })
  }
```

This will update the `todo` list and also the text input state with an empty string so that new values can be added later.

To display the data, we use a dumb component whose only purpose is to display the to-do list. This component has nothing to do with Redux. You can find this dumb component inside `component/TodoList.js`

Finally, when we run our application, we will find the result shown in Figure 3-8 in the simulator.

Figure 3-8. *Showing the to-do list on an iPhone*

As you saw, there is some work involved in using Redux along with your application, and as with any new piece of technology or new pattern, developers should always ask this: Why should I use it in the first place?"

It might be a little complicated to understand and implement something with Redux, but once you understand the fundamentals, it provides many advantages, including these:

- *Expected outcomes:* With Redux there is no confusion about where to locate our one source of truth; that will always be the store.

- *Maintainability and organization of code:* With a strict structure in place and predictable outcomes, maintaining the code becomes easier. Redux is also particular about how the code should be organized, and this becomes pivotal in maintaining the source code as an application becomes large.

- *Tools:* With developer tools, developers can track what's happening in the application in real time.

- *Community:* Redux is not something that has just appeared; it has indeed passed the test of time. The community is flourishing, and you can easily get support and regular updates for the library.

- *Ease of testing:* Redux functions by design are small, pure, and isolated, which makes them perfect candidates to for which to write tests. Redux apps automatically make testing easy for the application.

Summary

In this chapter you learned about the Flux pattern, how it differs, and how it solves a fundamental problem differently from the traditional MVC pattern. We also looked closer at Flux core concepts. Next, you learned about the successor of Flux, Redux, its core concepts, benefits, and how to use it with React Native applications, which will be useful in real-world applications and in the upcoming chapters. Chapter 4 covers how to create UIs and navigation in React Native apps. Finally, you learn how to use animation in your views.

CHAPTER 4

Canvas, Brush, and Paint: Working with the User Interface

A user interface is the process of shifting from chaotic complexity to elegant simplicity.

—Akshat Paul

Chapter 3 introduced React Native state management using Flux and Redux, and you created your first React Native application. Now that you have a skeleton for your project, let's fill it out with a stunning UI. This chapter covers the following topics:

- React Navigation
- Flexbox
- TouchableHighlight
- ListView
- ScrollView
- Animations

Any experienced software professional will agree: The success of an app depends on the fact that it not only works flawlessly, but also looks great. Therefore, a great UI can make a huge difference in the success of your app.

© Akshat Paul and Abhishek Nalwaya 2019
A. Paul and A. Nalwaya, *React Native for Mobile Development*, https://doi.org/10.1007/978-1-4842-4454-8_4

The layout system is a fundamental concept that needs to be mastered to create great applications. Let's begin by understanding how to navigate within iOS and Android applications using React Native.

React Navigation

React Navigation is one of the popular JavaScript libraries for handling routing in React Native applications. iOS and Android have different ways to handle navigation, and react-navigation takes care of this for both platforms.

To start, we need to install the react-navigation npm module. Let's build on the HouseShare application we created in Chapter 2:

```
yarn add react-navigation
```

Let's create a screen that we will use to render through react-navigation. We will create a new folder with the name screens in the root directory and create a HomeScreen.js file inside the same folder. Add the following code in Homescreen.js:

```
import React from 'react';
import { StyleSheet, Text, View, Button } from 'react-native';

export default class HomeScreen extends React.Component {
  render() {
    return (
      <View style={styles.home}>
      <Text>Home Screen</Text>
      </View>
    );
  }
}

const styles = StyleSheet.create({
  home: {
    flex: 1,
    alignItems: 'center',
    justifyContent: 'center',
  },
});
```

We just created a HomeScreen React component, which shows text that is center aligned. Because this component exported from App.js is the entry point for your app and other components descend from it, we need to update App.js to include Navigation. Let's import the HomeScreen component in App.js and update the following code:

```
import React from 'react';
import { StyleSheet, Text, View } from 'react-native';
import { createStackNavigator } from 'react-navigation';
import HomeScreen from './screens/HomeScreen';

const AppNavigator = createStackNavigator({
  Home: {
    screen: HomeScreen
  },
});

export default class App extends React.Component {
  render() {
    return <AppNavigator />;
  }
}
```

Now run the app in a simulator:

```
$ yarn start
```

Figure 4-1 shows a HomeScreen rendered using react-navigation. We have used createStackNavigator, which returns a React component.

Figure 4-1. *HomeScreen React component loaded*

createStackNavigator takes a route configuration object and because it returns a React component, we can use this in the App component. It provides a way for your app to transition between components and manage navigation history, gestures, and animations, which is natively provided in Android and iOS.

Right now, we have used just the HomeScreen component. Let's add one more screen and use react-navigation to route to this new screen.

Let's create the AboutScreen.js component inside the screens folder and add the following code in it:

```
import React from 'react';
import { StyleSheet, Text, View } from 'react-native';
```

```
export default AboutScreen = () => {
    return (
      <View style={styles.about}>
        <Text>About Screen</Text>
      </View>
    );
}

const styles = StyleSheet.create({
  about: {
    flex: 1,
    alignItems: 'center',
    justifyContent: 'center',
  },
});
```

Here we have created a stateless React component, which shows text that is center aligned. Now we update StackNavigator to add this screen to the stack. Open App.js and add this route:

```
const AppNavigator = createStackNavigator({
  Home: {
    screen: HomeScreen
  },
  About: {
    screen: AboutScreen
  }},
  {
   initialRouteName: 'Home',
  }
);

export default class App extends React.Component {
  render() {
    return <AppNavigator />;
  }
}
```

We have also defined an initalRouteName, which will be opened as the first screen of the application. Now let's add a button to HomeScreen. The purpose of this button will be to traverse to AboutScreen when clicked. We will do this by using react-navigation prop this.props.navigation.navigate('TargetRoute'), which is automatically injected into your component. Let's update HomeScreen.js with the following code:

```javascript
import React from 'react';
import { StyleSheet, Text, View, Button } from 'react-native';

export default class HomeScreen extends React.Component {
  static navigationOptions = {
    title: 'Welcome',
  };
  render() {
    const { navigate } = this.props.navigation;
    return (
      <View style={styles.home}>
      <Text>Home Screen</Text>
      <Button
        title="Go About Page"
        onPress={() =>
          navigate('About')
        }
      />
      </View>
    );
  }
}

const styles = StyleSheet.create({
  home: {
    flex: 1,
    alignItems: 'center',
    justifyContent: 'center',
  },
});
```

Let's test our app in in the simulator:

```
$ yarn start
```

Figure 4-2 shows the two screens and how users can navigate between them.

Figure 4-2. *Navigating using React Navigation*

We have used `createStackNavigator`, which has created screens as a stack that can be navigated with the back button at the top. It manages a stack of screens to provide a drill-down interface for hierarchical content.

Let's customize the header next. You can do this on a global level as well as at the screen level. We start with the global level. Update App.js with

```
}
 }
}
);
```

Run the app. Figure 4-3 shows the updated header styling for all the screens, but you can override this for a specific screen by adding this in a component as a static variable.

Figure 4-3. *Header styling updated*

NavigatorIOS

If you are only targeting iOS you can also use NavigatorIOS. It wraps UIKit navigation and allows you to add a backswipe feature to your app. NavigatorIOS manages a stack of view controllers to provide a drill-down interface for hierarchical content. Now that we know what NavigatorIOS does, let's implement it in our project.

Note   NavigatorIOS helps with the most basic iOS routing. A route is an object that describes each view in the navigator.

```
<NavigatorIOS
  initialRoute={{
    component: HomeScreen,
    title: 'Title for screen',
    passProps: {myProp: 'foo'},
  }}
/>
```

We have done a little bit of styling in this section, which might be something new for you if you come from a grid-layout background. React Native uses Flexbox for styling, which is discussed in detail next.

Flexbox

In creating the layout in the previous example, you must have seen the `flex` property mentioned in the styles. This appears because React Native apps use the Flexbox layout model.

The React Native Flexbox layout model is inspired by the CSS Flex Box Layout from CSS3. The React Native team has rewritten this feature specifically for iOS. The main idea behind Flexbox is being able to create a layout without worrying about different screen sizes or device orientation. A flex container expands items to fill available free space or shrinks them to prevent overflow. Let's get some basic knowledge of Flexbox to expedite our layout development. First, let's update the view in `HomeScreen.js`:

```
Houseshare/screens/HomeScreen.js
export default class HomeScreen extends React.Component {
  static navigationOptions = {
    title: 'House Share',
  };
  render() {
    const { navigate } = this.props.navigation;
```

```
  return (
    <View style={styles.container}>
      <View style={styles.topBox} />
      <View style={styles.bottomBox} />
    </View>
  );
  }
}
```

We have created one main view with a style container and two subviews with the styles topBox and bottomBox. Now, let's create the styles:

```
var styles = StyleSheet.create({
  container: {
    flex: 1,
    flexDirection: 'column'
  },
  topBox: {
      flex: 2,
      backgroundColor: '#CCE5FF'
  },
  bottomBox: {
      flex: 1,
      backgroundColor: '#FFFFCC'
  }
});
```

Turn back to the simulator and refresh the view using Command + R. Now, rotate the simulator, and you will see it automatically adjust the size of these colored boxes. Figure 4-4 shows the simulator in portrait mode.

Figure 4-4. *Screen in portrait mode*

Let's change the simulator to landscape mode (see Figure 4-5). This can be done easily using Command + Right/Left arrow key (⌘ + Left Arrow). You can see how the box has adjusted its size, and how the title adjusted its width to use all the available space. Thanks to Flexbox, a pretty laborious task is simplified.

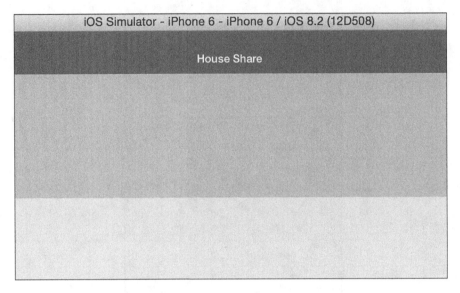

Figure 4-5. *Screen in landscape mode*

Now, let's review the flex properties Flex-direction and flex.

flexDirection

Flexbox is a single-direction layout concept. flexDirection allows you to define the direction in which the child elements are going to flow. It can have two values, row and column. In the previous example we used column. Let's change it to row here:

```
container: {
    flex: 1,
    flexDirection: 'row'
}
```

Turn back to the simulator and refresh the view with Command + R (see Figure 4-6).

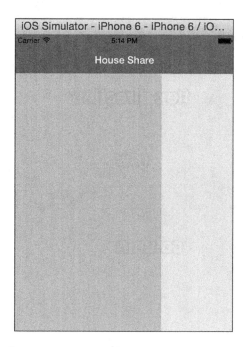

Figure 4-6. *Changing the orientation of the box*

You can see how the orientation of the box has changed. Now change the property `flexDirection` to `column` (see Figure 4-7).

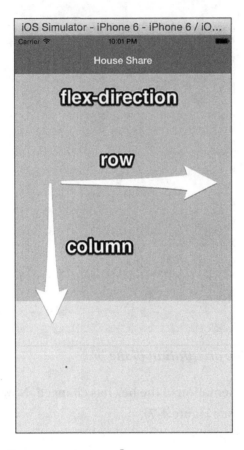

Figure 4-7. *Changing the property to* `column`

Flex

You must have seen the `flex` value in the stylesheet; it can be either integers or decimals, indicating the relative size of the box:

```
container: {
    flex: 1,
    flexDirection: 'column'
  },

topBox: {
        flex: 2,
        backgroundColor: '#CCE5FF',
    },
```

```
bottomBox: {
    flex: 1,
    backgroundColor: '#FFFFCC'
}
```

Our view says:

```
<View style={styles.container}>
    <View style={styles.topBox} />
    <View style={styles.bottomBox} />
</View>
```

flex thus defines the size percentage for the box. We can see that the container has two views inside, topBox and bottomBox, with flex values of 2 and 1, respectively (see Figure 4-8).

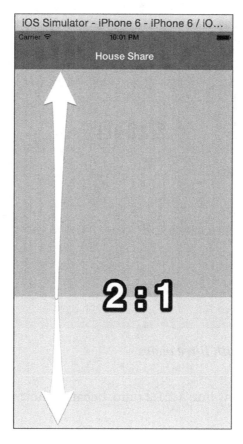

Figure 4-8. *Container in 2:1 ratio*

Now, update the view and add one topBox view inside the container view:

```
<View style={styles.container}>
    <View style={styles.topBox} />
    <View style={styles.bottomBox} />
    <View style={styles.topBox} />
</View>
```

Refresh the view. The container has three views now: topBox, bottomBox, and then topBox again (see Figure 4-9).

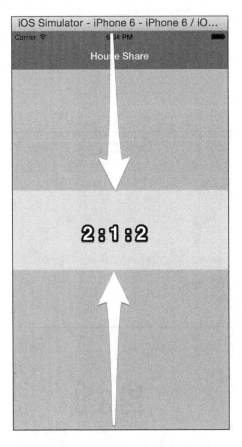

Figure 4-9. *Container with three views*

This will divide the view into a 2:1:2 ratio, because their flex values are in the ratio 2:1:2.

To get a better sense of how this works, let's change the flex values and see how that changes our screen. Let's change the flex value of topBox to 1. Update the CSS to:

```
container: {
    flex: 1,
    flexDirection: 'column'
  },

topBox: {
      flex: 1,
      backgroundColor: '#CCE5FF',
    },
    bottomBox: {
      flex: 1,
      backgroundColor: '#FFFFCC'
    }
```

Refresh the view to see the changes, as shown in Figure 4-10.

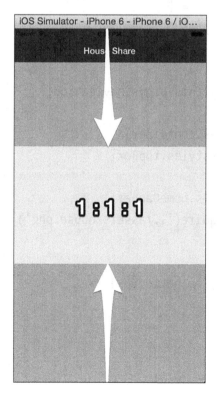

Figure 4-10. *View in 1:1:1 ratio*

We can see that now the screen is divided in a ratio of 1:1:1, because the flex values of the views are in a ratio of 1:1:1. With Flexbox, it is easy to create layouts that can resize according to screen size and orientation. This is just an introduction to Flexbox; we explain more properties throughout the book as and when needed. You can also find more options at https://facebook.github.io/react-native/docs/flexbox.html.

Images

React Native has a built-in component, Image, that will help us to display images, including network images, temporary local images, and also images from a local disk, such as the Camera Roll. To start, we display local images.

Copy a home image from the assets folder and update HomeScreen.js:

```
import React from 'react';
import { StyleSheet, Text, View, Button, Image} from 'react-native';

export default class HomeScreen extends React.Component {
  static navigationOptions = {
    title: 'House Share',
  };
  render() {
    const { navigate } = this.props.navigation;
    return (
      <View style={styles.container}>
          <View style={styles.topBox} >
              <Image
            style={styles.homeBanner}
            source={require('../assets/house.png')}
        />
          </View>
        <View style={styles.bottomBox} />
      </View>
    );
  }
}
```

```
const styles = StyleSheet.create({
  container: {
  flex: 1,
  flexDirection: 'column'
  },

 topBox: {
     flex: 1,
     backgroundColor: '#C0C0C0'
  },
  bottomBox: {
     flex: 2,
     backgroundColor: '#fff'
  },
  homeBanner: {
    bottom:0,
    flex: 1,
  alignSelf: 'stretch',
  width: undefined,
  height: undefined,
  }
});
```

Now run the simulator. The results are shown in Figure 4-11.

Figure 4-11. *Adding images*

We can also give any server image URL as the source, and the Image component will take care of loading it from the network. For a different screen size you can also give images of a different density by using the @2x and @3x suffixes in the same folder. We will load an image from a server later in this chapter.

TouchableHighlight

Touch is one of the ways to interact with a view in an application. TouchableHighlight is a React Native component that helps us create clickable views that give a proper response in the event of a touch. To understand TouchableHighlight with an example, let's continue building our app by adding one more view to list the housing options. This will be done by clicking on the show house image, which will redirect to another component.

Let's add the TouchableHighlight component, making the image we have added into a clickable view. Update the view, remove View, and add TouchableHighlight in HomeScreen.js:

```
<View style={styles.container}>
        <TouchableHighlight style={styles.topBox} onPress={() =>
          navigate('HomeListScreen')}>
            <Image
          style={styles.homeBanner}
          source={require('../assets/house.png')}
        />
        </TouchableHighlight>
      <View style={styles.bottomBox} />
    </View>
```

Let us review what we have done here; we have added an onPress attribute to our TouchableHighlight component for the List Properties section. Whenever someone presses the List Properties image, it calls navigate('HomeListScreen').

We have also created a HomeListScreen.js page in the screens folder:

```
import React from 'react';
import { Text, View} from 'react-native';

export default HomeListScreen = () => {
    return (
      <View>
      <Text> Home List Screen </Text>
      </View>

    );
}
```

Finally, update this page in App.js:

```
import HomeListScreen from './screens/HomeListScreen';

const AppNavigator = createStackNavigator({
  Home: {
    screen: HomeScreen
  },
```

```
  About: {
    screen: AboutScreen
  },
  HomeListScreen: {
    screen: HomeListScreen
  }
  },
  {
   initialRouteName: 'Home',
   navigationOptions: {
   headerStyle: {
     backgroundColor: '#48BBEC',
   },
   headerTintColor: '#fff',
   headerTitleStyle: {
     fontWeight: 'bold',
   }
 }
}
);
```

Refresh the app in the simulator and you'll see the image. When you click that image the new page shown in Figure 4-12 appears.

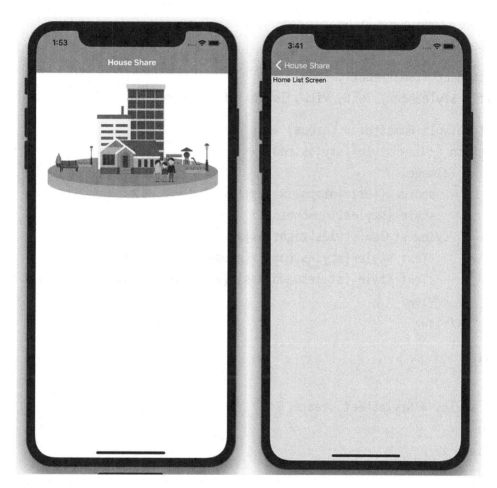

Figure 4-12. *Clickable View with* `TouchableHighlight`

Now we will load the image from a server and then create a nice-looking property view. This will look something like Figure 4-13.

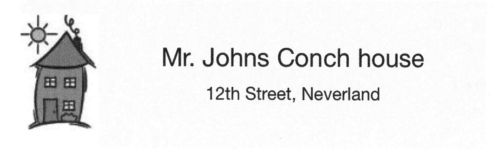

Figure 4-13. *Property name and address*

Create a components folder in the root folder and create HouseItem.js inside the components folder:

```
import React from 'react';
import { StyleSheet, Text, View, Image } from 'react-native';

export default HomeItem = (props) => {
    return (<View style={styles.row} >
            <Image
              source={{uri: props.images}}
              style={styles.thumbnail}/>
            <View style={styles.rightBox}>
              <Text style={styles.name}>{props.name}</Text>
              <Text style={styles.address}>{props.address}</Text>
            </View>
          </View>

    );
}

const styles = StyleSheet.create({
  row: {
    flex: 1,
    flexDirection: 'row',
    alignItems: 'center',
    backgroundColor: '#F5FCFF',
    borderWidth: 1,
    borderColor: '#d6d7da',
  },
  thumbnail: {
    width: 53,
    height: 81,
  },
  rightBox: {
    flex: 1,
  },
```

```
  name: {
    fontSize: 20,
    marginBottom: 8,
    textAlign: 'center',
  },
  address: {
    textAlign: 'center',
  },
});
```

Now open HomeListScreen.js:

```
HouseShare/screens/HomeScreen.js
import React from 'react';
import { Text, View} from 'react-native';
import HouseItem from '../components/HouseItem';

export default HomeListScreen = () => {
    return (
      <HouseItem name=" Mr. Johns Conch house" address=" 12th Street,
      Neverland" images='http://hmp.me/ol5'/>
    );
}
```

Let's refresh our application in the iOS simulator to see the changes (see Figure 4-14).

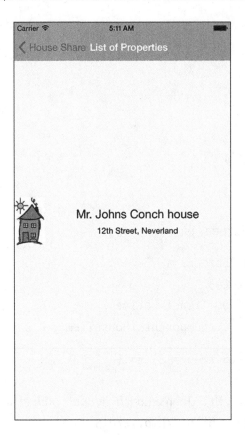

Figure 4-14. Thumbnail image with property name and address

ListView

In the previous section, we populated one element. In this section, we populate a list of data using ListView. Before we embark on that, let's learn a bit more about a different way to show the ListView component in React Native. React Native has two components: FlatList and SectionList.

FlatList is a component designed for populating vertically scrolling lists of dynamic data. The minimal steps are to create a FlatList data source and populate it with an array of data similar to the native TableView data source.

ListView looks very similar to TableView, but the implementation doesn't actually use TableView. Rather, it uses ScrollView behind the scenes. Features like swipe to delete, reordering, and so on, cannot be used directly through ListView.

We will show the list of house address, as an example of the most common representation of data in mobile devices. With our HouseShare app, we will create a table view showing a list of properties, each of which has a thumbnail image to the left side. The rest of the details should appear next to it.

To keep things simple for this chapter, we mock up data instead of pulling them from some external service (later, you will learn how to pull the same data from an external API). With these data, we will show the name of the property, its address, and a thumbnail picture. Replace the following code in HouseListScreen.js:

HouseShare/screens/HomeListScreen.js

```
import React from 'react';
import { Text, View, FlatList } from 'react-native';
import HouseItem from '../components/HouseItem';

const MOCK_DATA = [
  { name: 'Mr. Johns Conch house', address: '12th Street, Neverland',
  images:  'http://hmp.me/ol5'},
  {name: 'Mr. Pauls Mansion', address: '625, Sec-5,  Ingsoc',
  images:  'http://hmp.me/ol6'},
  {name: 'Mr. Nalwayas Villa', address: '11, Heights, Oceania',
  images:  'http://hmp.me/ol7'},
  {name: 'Mr. Johns Conch house', address: '12th Street, Neverland',
  images:  'http://hmp.me/ol5'},
  {name: 'Mr. Pauls Mansion', address: '625, Sec-5,  Ingsoc', images:
  'http://hmp.me/ol6'},
  {name: 'Mr. Nalwayas Villa', address: '11, Heights, Oceania', images:
  'http://hmp.me/ol7'},
  {name: 'Mr. Johns Conch house', address: '12th Street, Neverland',
  images: 'http://hmp.me/ol5'},
  {name: 'Mr. Pauls Mansion', address: '625, Sec-5,  Ingsoc', images:
  'http://hmp.me/ol6'},
  {name: 'Mr. Nalwayas Villa', address: '11, Heights, Oceania', images:
  'http://hmp.me/ol7'}
];
```

```
export default HomeListScreen = () => {

    return (
      <FlatList
        data={MOCK_DATA}
        renderItem={({item}) => <HouseItem {...item}/>}
        keyExtractor={(item, index) => index.toString()}
        />
    );
}
```

Refresh your application in the simulator to see the updated view, as shown in Figure 4-15.

Figure 4-15. *Scrollable addresses*

Great! Now we have a list of properties that we can scroll through. Let's review the implementation now:

```
import { Text, View, FlatList } from 'react-native';
import HouseItem from '../components/HouseItem';
```

We have once again specified what all components will be using in this section. There is a new component added, FlatList.

Next, we created MOCK_DATA, which is an array of hashes with property details:

```
var MOCK_DATA =[
  {name: 'Mr. Johns Conch house', address: '12th Street, Neverland',
  images: {thumbnail: 'http://hmp.me/ol5'}},
  {name: 'Mr. Pauls Mansion', address: '625, Sec-5,  Ingsoc', images:
  {thumbnail: 'http://hmp.me/ol6'}},
  {name: 'Mr. Nalwayas Villa', address: '11, Heights, Oceania', images:
  {thumbnail: 'http://hmp.me/ol7'}},
  {name: 'Mr. Johns Conch house', address: '12th Street, Neverland',
  images: {thumbnail: 'http://hmp.me/ol5'}},
  {name: 'Mr. Pauls Mansion', address: '625, Sec-5,  Ingsoc', images:
  {thumbnail: 'http://hmp.me/ol6'}},
  {name: 'Mr. Nalwayas Villa', address: '11, Heights, Oceania', images:
  {thumbnail: 'http://hmp.me/ol7'}},
  {name: 'Mr. Johns Conch house', address: '12th Street, Neverland',
  images: {thumbnail: 'http://hmp.me/ol5'}},
  {name: 'Mr. Pauls Mansion', address: '625, Sec-5,  Ingsoc', images:
  {thumbnail: 'http://hmp.me/ol6'}},
  {name: 'Mr. Nalwayas Villa', address: '11, Heights, Oceania', images:
  {thumbnail: 'http://hmp.me/ol7'}}
];
```

In this code we added more entries to create a FlatList view. Now, let's look at the changes we made in our component:

```
<FlatList
      data={MOCK_DATA}
      renderItem={({item}) => <HouseItem {...item}/>}
      keyExtractor={(item, index) => index.toString()}
      />
```

We have passed three props in the FlatList component: data, renderItem, and keyExtractor:

- data is the source of information for the list.

- renderItem takes one item from the source and returns a formatted component to render.

- keyExtractor tells the list to use the IDs for the React keys instead of the default key property.

ScrollView

Although we are not using ScrollView in our HouseShare application, it can be used as an alternate way to populate a list just like we used ListView. ScrollView is one of the most versatile and useful controls, as it is a great way to list content that is greater in size than the screen size.

We can add a basic ScrollView by using the following code:

```
<ScrollView>
        <Text>Scroll me plz</Text>
        <Image source={{uri: "'http://hmp.me/ol5", width: 64, height: 64}} />
                <Image source={{uri: "'http://hmp.me/ol5", width: 64,
                height: 64}} />
        <Image source={{uri: "'http://hmp.me/ol5", width: 64, height: 64}} />
        <Image source={{uri: "'http://hmp.me/ol5", width: 64, height: 64}} />
        <Image source={{uri: "'http://hmp.me/ol5", width: 64, height: 64}} />
        <Image source={{uri: "'http://hmp.me/ol5", width: 64, height: 64}} />
        <Image source={{uri: "'http://hmp.me/ol5", width: 64, height: 64}} />
</ScrollView>
```

This is basic ScrollView; if we want to scroll horizontally and we want to lock that direction, we can do so with the following:

```
<ScrollView
        horizontal={true}
        directionalLockEnabled={true}
                >
```

There are many other options available with `ScrollView`; for documentation and examples, you can visit `https://facebook.github.io/react-native/docs/scrollview.html`.

<ScrollView> vs. <FlatList>

`ScrollView` is easy to use and it simply renders all its React child components at once, whereas `FlatList` renders items lazily, just when they are about to appear, and removes items that scroll far off screen to save memory and processing time.

Animations

Animations are crucial when it comes to creating a good user experience. If you think of any popular mobile app, you will likely find animation at the center of an immersive user experience. React Native provides an animation API to perform different types of animations with ease.

There are many different `Animated` methods that you can use to create animations, including these:

- `Animated.timing()`: Animation based on time range.

- `Animated.decay()`: Animation starts with an initial velocity and gradually slows to a stop.

- `Animated.spring()`: This is a simple single-spring physics model that tracks velocity state to create fluid motions as the `toValue` updates, and can be chained together.

- `Animated.parallel()`: This starts an array of animations all at the same time.

- `Animated.sequence()`: We can perform an array of animations in order, waiting for each to complete before starting the next.

Let's add some animation in our HouseShare app. Create a file `FadeInView.js` in the `components` folder and add the following code:

```
HouseShare/components/FadeInView.js
import React from 'react';
import { Animated, Text, View } from 'react-native';
```

```
export default  class FadeInView extends React.Component {
  state = {
    fadeAnim: new Animated.Value(0),
  }

  componentDidMount() {
    Animated.timing(
      this.state.fadeAnim,
      {
        toValue: 1,
        duration: 4000,
      }
    ).start();
  }

  render() {
    let { fadeAnim } = this.state;

    return (
      <Animated.View
        style={{
          ...this.props.style,
          opacity: fadeAnim,
        }}
      >
        {this.props.children}
      </Animated.View>
    );
  }
}
```

We have defined a state this.state.fadeAnim, which is the opacity value. We
have defined this value from 0 as initial state. The opacity property on the View is
then mapped to this animated value. We have used Animated.timing to increase the

opacity from 0 to 1 in 4,000 ms. Next we wrap `FadeInView` with any `View` and it can `FadeIn` that `View` for 4,000 ms. Let's open `HomeItem.js` and replace the root `View` with `FadeInView`, as shown:

```
HouseShare/components/HomeItem.js
<FadeInView style={styles.row} >
        <Image
          source={{uri: props.images}}
          style={styles.thumbnail}/>
        <View style={styles.rightBox}>
          <Text style={styles.name}>{props.name}</Text>
          <Text style={styles.address}>{props.address}</Text>
        </View>
    </FadeInView>
```

Run the app and you can see the `FadeIn` animation on the Home List page. There are several different configurations available, which are documented at `https://facebook.github.io/react-native/docs/animated#configuring-animations`.

Summary

In this chapter, we learned some of the fundamentals that are essential for creating a stunning user experience. We covered the following:

- React Navigation

- NavigatorIOS for back-swipe functionality across apps

- The Flexbox layout model

- `TouchableHighlight`, a wrapper for making views respond properly to touches

- Using `ListView` for efficient scrolling of vertical lists

- Using `ScrollView` for listing content larger than the screen size

- Using the Animate API of React Native to animate a `View`.

The next chapter covers different device capabilities like MapView, AsyncStorage, Native Alert, WebView, and deep linking.

CHAPTER 5

Exploring Device Capabilities

Software will give you respect, but hardware will give you the power.

—Akshat Paul

Mobile devices are not just limited to making phone calls; they are some of the most advanced pieces of consumer technology ever invented. Their real power lies in the various capabilities that reside in a smartphone. The iOS and Android platforms allow us to use various device features to make a more captivating application experience for our users. This chapter explores the following device capabilities:

- MapView and GeoLocation

- AsyncStorage

- Native Alert

- WebView

- Deep linking

MapView and GeoLocation

In this section, we will learn how to use iOS and Android location services with a React Native application. Location services are used very often in many popular apps, especially in travel, navigation, ride sharing, and so on. This single feature significantly improves the user experience and the bonus is that it's very easy to implement.

© Akshat Paul and Abhishek Nalwaya 2019
A. Paul and A. Nalwaya, *React Native for Mobile Development*, https://doi.org/10.1007/978-1-4842-4454-8_5

Before we learn about GeoLocation, though, we need to learn about MapView, which is essentially designed to show a location on a map. We use the react-native-maps npm module(https://www.npmjs.com/package/react-native-maps), which is a component for iOS and Android to show maps. Access your terminal to create an application to implement this capability:

```
$ expo init GeoLocationMaps
```

This creates a React Native app with Expo CLI. Next, add the react-native-maps npm module, using yarn:

```
$ yarn add react-native-maps
```

react-native-maps (https://github.com/react-community/react-native-maps) is one of the best modules for map views. It includes numerous customization options available to help you design the best possible experience with maps.

Because App.js is the entry point in a React Native app, update the following code in that file:

GeoLocationMaps/App.js

```
import React from 'react';
import { StyleSheet, Text, View } from 'react-native';
import MapView from 'react-native-maps';

export default class App extends React.Component {
  constructor(props) {
    super(props);
    this.state = {
      region: {
        latitude: 37.3230,
        longitude: -122.0322,
        latitudeDelta: 0.0922,
        longitudeDelta: 0.0922,
      }
    };
  }
```

```
render() {
    return (
        <MapView
        style={styles.container}
        initialRegion={this.state.region}
        / >
        );
    }
}

const styles = StyleSheet.create({
    container: {
        flex: 1,
    },
});
```

Now build your application by executing following the command, and open an iOS or Android simulator:

```
$ yarn start
```

You will see the map shown in Figure 5-1.

Figure 5-1. *GeoLocation MapView*

Reviewing the GeoLocationMap Code

Let's now understand what we have done in this part of our program.

```
import React from 'react';
import { StyleSheet, Text, View } from 'react-native';
import MapView from 'react-native-maps';
```

We have imported the MapView component from react-native-maps. Next, we used the MapView component to plot a map:

```
export default class App extends React.Component {
  constructor(props) {
    super(props);
    this.state = {
```

```
      region: {
        latitude: 37.3230,
        longitude: -122.0322,
        latitudeDelta: 0.0922,
        longitudeDelta: 0.0922,
      }
    };
  }
  render() {
    return (
      <MapView
      style={styles.container}
      initialRegion={this.state.region}
    / >
    );
  }
}
```

Here, we have set the initial state for the region with certain latitude, longitude, latitudeDelta, and longitudeDelta parameters, which will be later set when we render the function with the MapView component. In the MapView component, we are using the region state, which is supplied with latitude, longitude, longitudeDelta, and latitudeDelta. These should always be numbers (integer or float), as they help us plot a specific region on the map. Finally, we have added some style with Flex and registered our component.

iOS devices show Apple Maps by default. We can choose to use a different provider like Google. Update provider to google with this code:

```
<MapView
  style={styles.container}
  provider="google"
  initialRegion={this.state.region}
/ >
```

Now run the application. You can see that instead of Apple Maps, it loads Google Maps (Figure 5-2).

Figure 5-2. *GeoLocation with Google Maps*

There are numerous customization options available. You can check `https://github.com/react-community/react-native-maps/blob/master/docs/mapview.md` for more details.

Adding Annotation on a Map

Annotations provide a way to highlight specific coordinates on a map. This valuable information is commonly added for any mobile application using a **geolocation** feature. Let's add an annotation marker to our application and update initial state with the new state annotations, with parameters `latitude` and `longitude` for the marker.

```
constructor(props) {
  super(props);
  this.state = {
```

```
    region: {
      latitude: 37.3230,
      longitude: -122.0322,
      latitudeDelta: 0.0922,
      longitudeDelta: 0.0922,
    },
    coordinate: {
    latitude: 37.3230,
    longitude: -122.0322,
    },
  };
}
```

Now update the MapView component with the new prop called coordinate:

```
<MapView
  style={styles.container}
  provider="google"
  initialRegion={this.state.region}
>
  <Marker coordinate={this.state.coordinate} />
</MapView>
```

Refresh and observe the changes. You will see something like the screen shown in Figure 5-3.

Figure 5-3. *MapView with added parameters*

Displaying the Latitude and Longitude of the Current Location

In this final part of our geolocation application, we will display our present latitude and longitude on the screen. In the previous example, we had a constant location; in this part, we will move to our current location in real time. That sounds like something exciting, so let's start building it. There are two ways to check for the current location on our maps. One is to simply add `showsUserLocation={true}` to the `MapView` component. Another way is to use `NSLocationWhenInUseUsageDescription` geolocation. Let's try the first option. If you are using gelocation on an existing project, you need to update `NSLocationWhenInUseUsageDescription` in `info.plist` for iOS and `<uses-permission android:name="android.permission.ACCESS_FINE_LOCATION" />`

in AndroidManifest.xml for Android. Because we have created a project with Expo, which initially uses react-native init, gelocation is enabled by default.

Update the App.js Marker component with the following code:

```
<MapView
  style={styles.container}
  provider="google"
  showsUserLocation={true}
  initialRegion={this.state.region}
>
  <Marker coordinate={this.state.coordinate} />
</MapView>
```

Now refresh the application to load it on the iOS simulator and you will see something similar to Figure 5-4.

Figure 5-4. *Access location prompt*

If we allow this request, the map will move to the location we specified in our code; in this case it's Apple's headquarters in Cupertino, California (Figure 5-5).

Figure 5-5. *Moving to a specified map location in the code*

Now let's use the other method to get the user's current location, using the Geolocation API, which is extended from the Geolocation web spec (https:// developer.mozilla.org/en-US/docs/Web/API/Geolocation). Let's first update the ref for MapView to this.map, so that we can use it:

```
<MapView
    ref={ref => { this.map = ref; }}
    style={styles.container}
    provider="google"
    showsUserLocation={true}
```

```
    followUserLocation={true}
    loadingEnabled={true}
    initialRegion={this.state.region}
  >
  <Marker coordinate={this.state.coordinate} />
</MapView>
```

Now add `navigator.geolocation.watchPosition` in the same file:

```
componentDidMount() {
  navigator.geolocation.watchPosition(
    (position) => {
      console.log(position);
      this.map.animateToRegion({
        latitude: position.coords.latitude,
        longitude: position.coords.longitude,
        latitudeDelta: 0.005,
        longitudeDelta: 0.005
      });
    },
    (error) => console.log(error.message),
    { enableHighAccuracy: false, timeout: 200000, maximumAge: 1000 },
  );
}
```

Here, in `componentDidMount`, we get the current position from the `watchPosition` function in `navigator.geolocation`, which continuously checks for location because we'll need to get the location coordinates as the user moves. The Google Maps geolocation API has a `watchPosition` method that will help us get the location coordinates whenever they change. There are also other functions available like `getCurrentPosition`, which checks the current location just once when the app is refreshed (Figure 5-6).

Figure 5-6. *Map showing the current location*

Because we have a console log, we can see the position as it appears in the console, as shown in Figure 5-7.

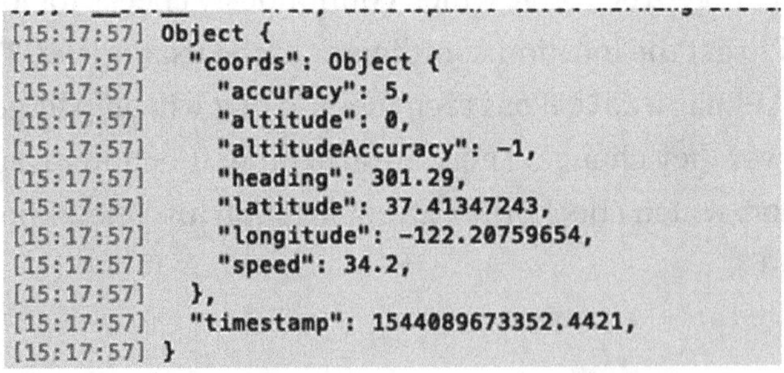

```
[15:17:57] Object {
[15:17:57]    "coords": Object {
[15:17:57]       "accuracy": 5,
[15:17:57]       "altitude": 0,
[15:17:57]       "altitudeAccuracy": -1,
[15:17:57]       "heading": 301.29,
[15:17:57]       "latitude": 37.41347243,
[15:17:57]       "longitude": -122.20759654,
[15:17:57]       "speed": 34.2,
[15:17:57]    },
[15:17:57]    "timestamp": 1544089673352.4421,
[15:17:57] }
```

Figure 5-7. *Current location displayed in the console log*

We can now see the current location. Next, let's try to change the location. To change a location, from the Simulator menu bar, select Debug ➤ Location ➤ Freeway Drive (see Figure 5-8). Freeway Drive will continuously change the simulator location.

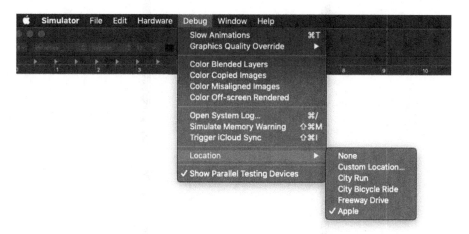

Figure 5-8.   *Change location using Simulator*

We can see that the location is changed dynamically in the app. Because we chose to use Freeway Drive, we can see that the location and maps continuously move along a freeway (Figure 5-9).

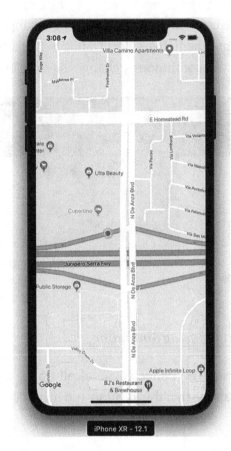

Figure 5-9. *Location changed to freeway*

AsyncStorage

AsyncStorage is a key/value-based storage system. It can be easily implemented and is globally available to the app. This persistence system is simple and asynchronous, and also a recommended way to store data. To create an AsyncStorage example application, execute the following command:

```
$expo init AsyncStorage
```

Add the following code in App.js:

```
import React from 'react';
import { StyleSheet, Text, View, TextInput, Button, AsyncStorage } from
'react-native';
```

```
export default class App extends React.Component {
  constructor(props) {
    super(props);
    this.state = {storedText: '', inputBoxText: ''}
}

  async componentDidMount() {
    this.setState({storedText: await this.retrieveData()});
  }
  onPressSave = async () => {
    try {
      await AsyncStorage.setItem('@AsyncStorageExample:someKey', this.
      state.inputBoxText);
      this.setState({storedText: this.state.inputBoxText})
    } catch (error) {
      console.log("Error in saving data");
    }
  }
  retrieveData = async () => {
    try {
      const value = await AsyncStorage.getItem('@AsyncStorageExample:someKey');
        return value;
      } catch (error) {
        console.log("Error in Fetching Data")
    }
  }
  render() {
    return (

        style={styles.textField}
        placeholder="Type here!"
        onChangeText={(text) => this.setState({inputBoxText: text})}
        />
        onPress={this.onPressSave}
        title="Save"
        color="blue"
```

```
            accessibilityLabel="Click will save to database"
            />
          Text from local Storage:
          {this.state.storedText}

      );
   }
}
const styles = StyleSheet.create({
  container: {
    flex: 1,
    backgroundColor: '#fff',
    alignItems: 'center',
    justifyContent: 'center',
  },
  header: {
    fontFamily: 'Georgia',
    fontSize: 20,
    fontWeight: 'bold',
    paddingTop: 40,
  },
  text: {
    fontFamily: 'Georgia',
    fontSize: 18,
    fontStyle: 'italic',
    paddingTop: 10,
  },
  textField: {
  height: 40,
  width: 300,
  borderColor: '#COCOCO',
  borderBottomWidth: 1,
  }
});
```

Let's build our application to see the results. You can enter the text in a text box as shown in Figure 5-10 and then click Save.

Figure 5-10. *Storage is updated*

Once that is done, refresh for the result shown in Figure 5-11.

Figure 5-11. *Text from the AsyncStorage mechanism*

This time the text below, "This text is from local storage," is coming from the AsyncStorage mechanism that we have put in place.

Reviewing the AsyncStorage Code

In this example, we have included the AsyncStorage default component in our list of components to be used for the sample application. Let's go through how exactly the code for this example works.

```
import React from 'react';
import { StyleSheet, Text, View, TextInput, Button, AsyncStorage } from
'react-native';
```

We use this AsyncStorage React component within our App component. Previously, we also specified a key that we will use with AsyncStorage.

Inside our App component we have set up `constructor` and `componentDidMount` methods and also created `onPressSave` and `retrieveData` methods. Let's discuss them one by one.

```
constructor(props) {
  super(props);
  this.state = {storedText: '', inputBoxText: ''}
}
```

In `constructor` we have specified blank values for `storedText` and `inputBoxText`, which we will keep updating as and when their state changes.

```
async componentDidMount() {
  this.setState({storedText: await this.retrieveData()});
}
```

`componentDidMount` is invoked only at the .time of initial rendering and is responsible for showing the text below "This text is from local storage," once we have updated the storage and refreshed the app again. We have used `async` and `await` for calling `retrieveData`, which means the execution will wait until the function is completely executed.

```
retrieveData = async () => {
  try {
    const value = await AsyncStorage.getItem('@AsyncStorageExample:someKey');
      return value;
  } catch (error) {
    console.log("Error in Fetching Data")
  }
}
```

The method `retrieveData` is used to retrieve the value stored in local storage. Calling `AsyncStorage.getItem` retrieves the value stored in local storage.

```
onPressSave = async () => {
  try {
    await AsyncStorage.setItem('@AsyncStorageExample:someKey', this.
    state.inputBoxText);
    this.setState({storedText: this.state.inputBoxText})
```

```
  } catch (error) {
    console.log("Error in saving data");
  }
}
```

Updating storage updates AsyncStorage values, which are persisted permanently.

```
render() {
  return (
    <View style={styles.container}>
        <TextInput
        style={styles.textField}
        placeholder="Type here!"
        onChangeText={(text) => this.setState({inputBoxText: text})}
      />
      <Button
        onPress={this.onPressSave}
        title="Save"
        color="blue"
        accessibilityLabel="Click will save to database"
        />
      <Text style={styles.header}>Text from local Storage:  </Text>
      <Text style={styles.text}>{this.state.storedText}</Text>
    </View>
  );
  }
}
```

The preceding code sets up various sections of our `AsyncStorageExample` component. Here, we can change a text input field to update the `textInputMessage` state. We also have an `onPress` prop for the `TouchableHighlight` component, which calls the `updatedStorage` method and persists the values permanently. In the end, we display the saved message by accessing the present state of the message.

```
const styles = StyleSheet.create({
  container: {
    flex: 1,
```

```
      backgroundColor: '#fff',
      alignItems: 'center',
      justifyContent: 'center',
    },
    header: {
      fontFamily: 'Georgia',
      fontSize: 20,
      fontWeight: 'bold',
      paddingTop: 40,
    },
    text: {
      fontFamily: 'Georgia',
      fontSize: 18,
      fontStyle: 'italic',
      paddingTop: 10,
    },
    textField: {
    height: 40,
    width: 300,
    borderColor: '#C0C0C0',
    borderBottomWidth: 1,
    }
});
```

Finally, we set up a UI style with some self-explanatory Flex settings and register our AsyncStorageExample component.

Native Alert

Alerts are used to provide important information to application users. Basic alerts consist of a dialog box with a specific title, message, and buttons. Occasionally alert boxes appear in an application to display a piece of important information. The buttons for an alert could either be a simple OK to proceed with the app, or OK, Cancel, Ask Me Later, and so on, which require the user to make a decision. Tapping this button could be linked to execute an inPress callback to execute a piece of code. By default an alert dialog box will have one button.

Let's create a project to understand more about Native Alert:

```
$ expo init NativeAlertApp
```

React Native provides the component `Alert` that works for both iOS and Android. Let's add a button that will open an alert box when clicked. Update `App.js` with the following code:

```
import React from 'react';
import { StyleSheet, Text, View, Button, Alert } from 'react-native';

export default class App extends React.Component {
  onPressButton1() {
    Alert.alert(
      'Alert Title',
      'Alert Message',
    )
  }
  render() {
    return (
      <View style={styles.container}>
        <Button
          onPress={this.onPressButton1}
          title="Button 1"
          color="#841584"
          accessibilityLabel="Learn more about Button 1"
        />
      </View>
    );
  }
}

const styles = StyleSheet.create({
  container: {
    flex: 1,
    backgroundColor: '#fff',
```

```
      alignItems: 'center',
      justifyContent: 'center',
  },
});
```

Let's build this application and test it in the simulator. Figure 5-12 shows the result.

Figure 5-12. *A button that will open an alert dialog box when clicked*

Tap the Button 1 button to see an alert box, as shown in the example in Figure 5-13.

Figure 5-13. *An alert dialog box*

Reviewing the NativeAlert Code

Now that you have created a new NativeAlert project, create a new `NativeAlert` component:

```
export default class App extends React.Component {
  onPressButton1() {
    Alert.alert(
      'Alert Title',
      'Alert Message',
    )
  }
  render() {
    return (
```

```
      <View style={styles.container}>
        <Button
          onPress={this.onPressButton1}
          title="Button 1"
          color="#841584"
          accessibilityLabel="Learn more about Button 1"
          />
      </View>
    );
  }
}
```

In the component `NativeAlert`, we have used `onPress` callback. The `Alert` method passes the strings `'Alert Title'` and `'Alert Message'`, which produce an alert dialog box containing a title, a message, and a button. Alert provides two methods, `alert` and `prompt`, as shown next. `Alert` creates and displays an alert, whereas `prompt` creates and displays a prompt to enter some text.

static alert(title: string, message?: string, buttons?: Array<{ text: ?string; onPress?: ?Function; }>, type?: string)

static prompt(title: string, value?: string, buttons?: Array<{ text: ?string; onPress?: ?Function; }>, callback?: Function)

Extending the NativeAlert Example

Now, to add some more buttons to the application, replace the following code for your `NativeAlert` component in `App.js`:

```
export default class App extends React.Component {
  onPressButton1() {
    Alert.alert(
      'Alert Title',
      'Alert Message',
    )
  }
  onPressButton2() {
```

```
    Alert.alert(
      'Alert Title',
      'Alert Message with Buttons',
      [
      {text: 'Button 1', onPress: () => console.log('Button 1 pressed')},
      {text: 'Button 2', onPress: () => console.log('Button 2 pressed')},
      {text: 'Cancel', onPress: () => console.log('Cancel Pressed'), style:
      'cancel'},
      ],
    )
  }
  render() {
    return (
      <View style={styles.container}>
        <Button
          onPress={this.onPressButton1}
          title="Button 1"
          color="#841584"
          accessibilityLabel="Learn more about Button 1"
          />
        <Button
          onPress={this.onPressButton2}
          title="Button 2"
          color="#841584"
          accessibilityLabel="Learn more about Button 2"
          />
      </View>
    );
  }
}
```

Let's refresh our view to see the changes made in Figure 5-14.

Figure 5-14. *Two buttons added on the screen*

Click Button 2 to view the result shown in Figure 5-15.

Figure 5-15. *Select Button 1, Button 2, or Cancel*

Tapping Button 2 fires an `onPress` callback that uses the `alert` method of `Alert` to set title, message, and buttons for our alert box. In this part of the `NativeAlert` component we have three buttons.

WebView

`WebView` is responsible for rendering web content in a Native view. That simply means `WebView` is an environment for loading a web URL inside your React Native application. `WebView` allows you to display web content as part of your app, but it lacks some of the features of fully developed browsers. Let's begin by generating an application for this:

```
$ react-native init WebViewApp
```

```
$yarn add react-native-webview
$react-native link react-native-webview
```

Now use one of the following commands to build the app. The first command is for an iOS simulator and the second one is for an Android simulator.

```
$react-native  run-ios
$react-native  run-android
```

Next, open App.js and replace its code with the following code:

```
import React, {Component} from 'react';
import {StyleSheet, SafeAreaView} from 'react-native';
import { WebView } from "react-native-webview";

export default class App extends Component<Props> {
  render() {
    return (
        <WebView
           style={{marginTop: 20}}
           source={{ uri: "https://www.wikipedia.org" }}
        />     );
  }
}

const styles = StyleSheet.create({
  container: {
    flex: 1,
    backgroundColor: '#F5FCFF',
  },
});
```

Let's build the application by running:

```
react-native  run-ios
```

The result is shown in Figure 5-16.

Figure 5-16. *WebView with a URL*

Reviewing the WebView Code

In this example, we have created a component App that returns a WebView. The following code creates a view with our desired URL loaded in the WebView.

```
export default class App extends Component<Props> {
  render() {
    return (
        <WebView
          style={{marginTop: 20}}
          source={{ uri: "https://www.wikipedia.org" }}
```

```
        />
    );
  }
}
}
```

Deep Linking

Deep linking is a technique that allows an app to be opened to a specific UI or resource, in response to some external event. The *deep* refers to the depth of the page in an app's hierarchical structure of pages. This is a very important feature for user engagement, as it also makes an app more responsive and capable of navigation to arbitrary content in response to external events like push notifications, e-mails, web links, and so on.

There are two ways of implementing deep linking: using a URL scheme or universal links. Although URL schemes are a well-known way of using deep linking, universal links are the new method Apple has implemented to easily connect your web page and your app under the same link. We implement URL schemes in our example that will handle external URIs. Let's suppose that we want a URI like myapp://article/4 to open our app and link straight into an article screen that shows article number 1.

We are using The React Native CLI instead of Expo CLI because we want to use customization in iOS and Android code. We can create the project using Expo and can then eject also.

```
$ react-native init DeepLinkApp
$ yarn add react-navigation
$ react-native link react-native-gesture-handler
```

After creating the project, we will add React Navigation and then use the link command to link React Native gesture handling. Create an src folder in the root folder and add the Article.js and Home.js files. Next, add following code in Home.js:

```
import React from 'react';
import { Text } from 'react-native';

class Home extends React.Component {
  static navigationOptions = {
    title: 'Home',
  };
```

```
  render() {
    return <Text>Hello from Home!</Text>;
  }
}

export default Home;
```

We have created a simple React component that rendered Text Hello from Home!. We next create a file Article.js in the src folder and add the following code:

```
import React from 'react';
import { Text } from 'react-native';

class Article extends React.Component {
  static navigationOptions = {
    title: 'Article',
  };

  render() {
    const { id } = this.props.navigation.state.params;
    return <Text>Hello from Article {id}!</Text>;
  }
}

export default Article;
```

We have now created two components, Home.js and Article.js, and we can add this in React Navigation routes. Open App.js and update the following code:

```
import React, {Component} from 'react';
import {Platform, StyleSheet, Text, View} from 'react-native';
import { createAppContainer, createStackNavigator} from "react-navigation";

import Home from './src/Home';
import Article from './src/Article';

const AppNavigator = createStackNavigator({
  Home: { screen: Home },
  Article: { screen: Article, path: 'article/:id', },
},
```

```
{
    initialRouteName: "Home"
 }
);
const prefix = Platform.OS == 'android' ? 'myapp://myapp/' : 'myapp://';
const App = createAppContainer(AppNavigator)
const MainApp = () => <App uriPrefix={prefix} />;
export default MainApp;
```

We have thus far created React Navigation and created routes for two pages. We have configured our `navigation` container to extract the path from the app's incoming URI. On Android, the URI prefix typically contains a host in addition to the scheme, so we have used `myapp://myapp/`.

Now we have to write custom code for iOS and Android. First, open the iOS project in the iOS folder by clicking `DeepLinkApp.xcodeproj`. Select the project title from the folder list and navigate to the Info tab as shown in Figure 5-17. Scroll down to the URL Types section and add one. For the new URL type, set the Identifier to `mychat` and the URL Scheme to `mychat`.

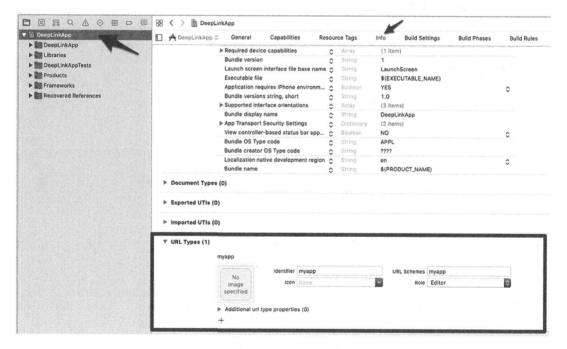

Figure 5-17. *Deep linking using Xcode*

135

Open AppDelegate.m in the root folder and add the following code before @end.

```
- (BOOL)application:(UIApplication *)application openURL:(NSURL *)url
  sourceApplication:(NSString *)sourceApplication annotation:(id)annotation
{
  return [RCTLinkingManager application:application openURL:url
                   sourceApplication:sourceApplication
                   annotation:annotation];
}
```

Now let's update the code for Android. To configure the external linking in Android, we need to create a new intent in the manifest. Open /src/main/AndroidManifest.xml to add the new intent-filter inside the MainActivity entry with a VIEW type action:

```
<intent-filter>
        <action android:name="android.intent.action.VIEW" />
        <category android:name="android.intent.category.DEFAULT" />
        <category android:name="android.intent.category.BROWSABLE" />
        <data android:scheme="myapp" android:host="myapp" />
    </intent-filter>
```

Let's start running the app, first with iOS:

```
$react-native run-ios
```

The result is shown in Figure 5-18.

Figure 5-18. *Running the app with iOS*

To test the DeepLink, open the Safari browser and type myapp://article/4. That will automatically open the app and open Article 4 (Figure 5-19).

Figure 5-19. *Traversing to the DeepLink page*

You can also open the DeepLink page by running this command on your terminal (Figure 5-20):

```
xcrun simctl openurl booted myapp://article/3
```

Figure 5-20. *Traversing to the DeepLink page*

Summary

This chapter covered various capabilities of iOS and Android devices using React Native. These capabilities helped us build features beyond just a UI. We learned how to use GeoLocation and loading maps for your app, AsyncStorage to persist data, Native alerts to share important info in your app, WebView to load HTML5 content, and finally deep linking.

Chapter 6 discusses how to interact with a back-end server because no real-world application is complete without connecting to a back end and consuming APIs.

CHAPTER 6

Communicating with Servers

Communication is everyone's panacea for everything.

—Tom Peters

After learning about the powers of device capabilities with many examples, it's time to get back to our SmartHouse application. So far, you have been populating your app locally with some dummy data, but no application can survive without communicating with a server. This chapter covers how to interact with network APIs. You will explore the following topics:

- `XMLHttpRequest`

- `WebSocket`

- `Fetch`

- Getting data from a server

- Posting data to a server

Earlier you were getting all the data from a dummy data object, which was static within your application. It's rare that any production application will work entirely with static data. Fortunately, React Native provides many ways to interact with network APIs. The following sections cover the ways the network stack is supported in React Native.

© Akshat Paul and Abhishek Nalwaya 2019
A. Paul and A. Nalwaya, *React Native for Mobile Development*, https://doi.org/10.1007/978-1-4842-4454-8_6

XMLHttpRequest

XMLHttpRequest is an API that provides the ability to transfer data between a client and a server. It provides an easy way to retrieve data from a URL without having to do a full-page refresh. In React Native, the XMLHttpRequest API is applied on top of the iOS networking APIs. This is the code snippet to use XMLHttpRequest.

```
var request = new XMLHttpRequest();
request.onreadystatechange = (e) => {
  if (request.readyState !== 4) {
    return;
  }

  if (request.status === 200) {
    console.log('success', request.responseText);
  } else {
    console.warn('error');
  }
};
request.open('GET', 'https://backendwebsite.com/endpointapi/');
request.send();
```

Using XMLHttpRequest is quite tedious. However, because it is compatible with the browser API, it lets you use third-party libraries directly from npm (e.g., Parse). For more information on this API, please refer to its documentation at https://developer. mozilla.org/en-US/docs/Web/API/XMLHttpRequest.

WebSocket

WebSocket is a protocol that provides full-duplex communication channels over a single Transmission Control Protocol (TCP) connection. With the WebSocket API it is possible to open two-way interactive communication. With this API, you can send messages to a server and receive event-driven responses without having to poll the server again and again for a reply. This is how the code looks for a WebSocket:

```
var ws = new WebSocket('ws://example.com/path');
```

```
ws.on('open', function() {
  // connection opened
  ws.send('example data');
});

ws.on('message', function(e) {
  // a message received
  console.log(e.data);
});

ws.on('error', function(e) {
  // an error occurred
  console.log(e.message);
});

ws.on('close', function(e) {
  // connection closed
  console.log(e.code, e.reason);
});
```

Fetch

Fetch is a popular networking API. It was created by a standard committee and has well-defined requests, responses, and the process to bind them. The following is an example of a post request with fetch:

```
fetch('https://example.com/endpoint/', {
  method: 'POST',
  headers: {
    'Accept': 'application/json',
    'Content-Type': 'application/json',
  },
  body: JSON.stringify({
    firstParam: 'yourValue',
    secondParam: 'otherValue',
  })
})
```

Fetch returns a promise because networking is an async operation, which means it will not wait for execution, so we can resolve using a then and catch block. We can get a response and error like this:

```
fetch('https:// example.com/endpoint')
  .then((response) => response.text())
  .then((responseText) => {
    console.log(responseText);
  })
  .catch((error) => {
    console.warn(error);
  });
```

Now that you know how to interact with network APIs, let's use one of the options, fetch, to get and post data to a server. To keep things simple, we have hosted a simple back-end server with restful APIs that you can consume for your application.

We will be using following the URLs to get and post data to a back-end server. For a quick test, you can use curl to see the response you get from making a request to these URLs.

Use this code to get an initial seed list of properties:

```
$curl 'http://www.akshatpaul.com/list-all-properties'
[
{
name: "Mr. Johns Conch house",
address: "12th Street, Neverland",
images: {
thumbnail: "http://hmp.me/ol5"
}
},
{
name: "Mr. Pauls Mansion",
address: "625, Sec-5, Ingsoc",
images: {
thumbnail: "http://hmp.me/ol6"
}
},
```

```
{
name: "Mr. Nalwayas Villa",
address: "11, Heights, Oceania",
images: {
thumbnail: "http://hmp.me/ol7"
}
}
]
```

To get the list of properties that the users have saved, run

```
$curl 'http://www.akshatpaul.com/list-properties'
```

You might see few results here that are created by other readers of this book.

To post data to the server to save a property we use the following API:

```
url: 'http://www.akshatpaul.com/properties'
```

Getting Data from a Server

First, let's get get some data from our back-end server that we use to populate the list of properties we have already added in our back-end server. So far this is getting populated from the JavaScript Object Notation (JSON) we have stored on our client application itself. Insert the following code into the HomeListScreen.js component:

```
import React from 'react';
import { FlatList }  from 'react-native';
import HouseItem from '../components/HouseItem';

export default class HomeListScreen extends React.Component {

  constructor(props) {
    super(props);
    this.state = {
      dataSource: null,
    }
  }
```

```
componentDidMount() {
  return fetch("https://www.akshatpaul.com/list-properties")
  .then ((response) => response.json() )
  .then ((responseJson) => {
    this.setState({
      dataSource: responseJson,
    })
  })
  .catch((error) => {
    console.log(error)

  });

}
render(){
    return (
      <FlatList
        data={this.state.dataSource}
        renderItem={(({item}) => <HouseItem {...item}/>}
        keyExtractor={(item, index) => index.toString()}
        />
    );
  }
}
```

Now, build or refresh the application and navigate to the of list of all the properties.
Figure 6-1 shows it loaded on an iOS simulator.

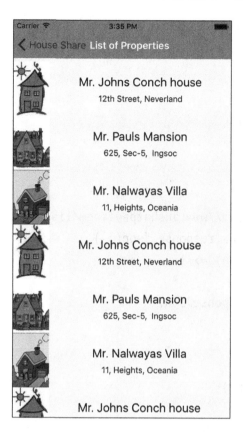

Figure 6-1. *Populating the app with static data fetched from a server*

All these data are coming from a back-end server. Let's walk through this code. Here, we first removed the MOCK_DATA, which is no longer required. We then modified the component type:

```
export default HomeListScreen = () => {
...
}
To
export default class HomeListScreen extends React.Component {
...
}
```

Earlier we had created a stateless component, but because we would like to use life cycle methods and maintain state, we have modified our stateless component to a state component.

Next, we added the following code in our `HomeListScreen` state component:

```
constructor(props) {
  super(props);
  this.state = {
    dataSource: null,
  }
}

componentDidMount() {
  return fetch("https://www.akshatpaul.com/list-properties")
  .then ((response) => response.json() )
  .then ((responseJson) => {
    this.setState({
      dataSource: responseJson,
    })
  })
  .catch((error) => {
    console.log(error)

  });

}
```

Here, we have created a `constructor` that sets the initial state for the `dataSource` property as `null`. This is the property that will store the data we will pull from a back-end server.

Next, we use a life cycle method `componentDidMount()`. We are making use of this life cycle method because we assume we would only be required to make a `get` call to the back-end API to get the list of properties once.

The structure of this request is straightforward: We use `fetch` to make a call that returns a promise. This promise is then resolved and we pass the response JSON to `dataSource` using the `setState` object.

Finally we have the placed catch() method to log any error. To load the data received from the back-end server, we are not making any changes in the earlier component except replacing `MOCK_DATA` with `this.state.dataSource`.

```
render(){
    return (
      <FlatList
        data={this.state.dataSource}
        renderItem={({item}) => <HouseItem {...item}/>}
        keyExtractor={(item, index) => index.toString()}
        />
    );
  }
```

Saving Data to a Server

In your housing application, so far you are able to get data from a back-end server.
This section shows you how to save data to a back-end API. For this we will create a
component to add new properties and make request to a back-end API to save the data.
For this purpose, we already have a back-end API ready to be consumed:

```
URL : http://www.akshatpaul.com/properties
```

Let's first add a button to HomeScreen that will navigate us to the Addproperty page.
Add the following code along with styling:

```
import React from 'react';
import { StyleSheet, Text, View, Image, TouchableHighlight } from
'react-native';

export default class HomeScreen extends React.Component {
  static navigationOptions = {
    title: 'House Share',
  };

  render() {
    const { navigate } = this.props.navigation;
```

```jsx
    return (
      <View style={styles.container}>
          <TouchableHighlight style={styles.topBox} onPress={() =>
            navigate('HomeListScreen')}>
              <Image
            style={styles.homeBanner}
            source={require('../assets/house.png')}
         />
        </TouchableHighlight>

        <TouchableHighlight style={styles.button}
          onPress={()=> navigate('AddNewProperty')}
          underlayColor='#99d9f4'>
          <Text style={styles.buttonText}>Add New Property</Text>
        </TouchableHighlight>

      <View style={styles.bottomBox} />
    </View>
  );
 }
}
const styles = StyleSheet.create({
  container: {
  flex: 1,
  flexDirection: 'column'
  },

 topBox: {
     flex: 1,
     backgroundColor: '#C0C0C0'
  },
  bottomBox: {
     flex: 2,
     backgroundColor: '#fff'
  },
```

```
homeBanner: {
  bottom:0,
  flex: 1,
alignSelf: 'stretch',
width: undefined,
height: undefined,
},
button: {
  flex: 1,
  backgroundColor: '#48BBEC',
  borderColor: '#48BBEC',
  borderWidth: 1,
  borderRadius: 8,
  alignSelf: 'stretch',
  justifyContent: 'center',
  margin: 10
},
buttonText: {
  fontSize: 18,
  color: 'white',
  alignSelf: 'center'
  }
});
```

Here, we have added a new button using the following code along with its styling:

```
<TouchableHighlight style={styles.button}
        onPress={()=> navigate('AddNewProperty')}
        underlayColor='#99d9f4'>
        <Text style={styles.buttonText}>Add New Property</Text>
    </TouchableHighlight>
```

```
button: {
  flex: 1,
  backgroundColor: '#48BBEC',
  borderColor: '#48BBEC',
  borderWidth: 1,
  borderRadius: 8,
  alignSelf: 'stretch',
  justifyContent: 'center',
  margin: 10
},
buttonText: {
  fontSize: 18,
  color: 'white',
  alignSelf: 'center'
}
```

We must also add a corresponding navigation route in `App.js` `createStackNavigator`:

```
const AppNavigator = createStackNavigator({
.
.
.
AddNewProperty: {
    screen: AddNewProperty
  }
.
.
};
```

Let's refresh to see the changes on the home screen (Figure 6-2).

Figure 6-2. *Showing the Add New Property button on the home page*

If we click Add New Property it will take us to a new screen that will be empty. Let's create a new file in the screens folder, AddNewProperty.js, and add the following code in it:

```
import React from 'react';
import { StyleSheet, Text, View, TouchableHighlight, TextInput, AlertIOS }
from 'react-native';
import HouseItem from '../components/HouseItem';

export default class AddNewProperty extends React.Component {
    constructor(props) {
        super(props);
        this.state = {
```

```
            name: "",
            address: ""
        }
    }

  onPressButtonPOST() {
      fetch('https://www.akshatpaul.com/properties', {
          method: 'POST',
          headers: {
          Accept: 'application/json',
          'Content-Type': 'application/json',
              },
          body: JSON.stringify({
              property: {
              name: this.state.name,
              address: this.state.address,
          }
      }),
  })
      .then((responseData) => {
          AlertIOS.alert(
              "Created"
          )
      })
      .done();
  }
render(){
    return (
        <View style={styles.container}>
        <TextInput style={styles.textBox} placeholder='name'
        onChangeText={(name) => this.setState({name})}
        value={this.state.name}  />
        <TextInput style={styles.textBox} placeholder='address'
        onChangeText={(address) => this.setState({address})}
        value={this.state.address} />
```

```
            <TouchableHighlight style={styles.button}
                onPress= {this.onPressButtonPOST.bind(this)}
                underlayColor='#99d9f4'>
                <Text style={styles.buttonText}>Add House</Text>
            </TouchableHighlight>
        </View>
    );
  }
}
var styles = StyleSheet.create({
    container: {
        flex: 1,
        flexDirection: 'column',
        justifyContent: 'center',
        alignItems: 'center',
        backgroundColor: '#F5FCFF',
    },
    textBox: {
        width:300,
        height:60,
        borderColor: 'gray',
        borderWidth: 1,
        alignSelf: 'center',
        marginTop: 10,
    },
    button: {

    height: 60,
    backgroundColor: '#48BBEC',
    borderColor: '#48BBEC',
    borderWidth: 1,
    borderRadius: 8,
    alignSelf: 'stretch',
    justifyContent: 'center',
    margin: 10
    },
```

```
buttonText: {
  fontSize: 18,
  color: 'white',
  alignSelf: 'center'
}
});
```

Let's step through this piece of code in detail. We created a new component, AddNewProperty, and added a constructor with two properties, name and address instantiated with an empty string:

```
constructor(props) {
    super(props);
    this.state = {
        name: "",
        address: ""
    }
  }
```

Next, we created the following component:

```
<View style={styles.container}>
    <TextInput style={styles.textBox} placeholder='name'
    onChangeText={(name) => this.setState({name})} value={this.state.
    name}  />
    <TextInput style={styles.textBox} placeholder='address'
    onChangeText={(address) => this.setState({address})} value={this.
    state.address} />
        <TouchableHighlight style={styles.button}
            onPress= {this._onPressButtonPOST.bind(this)}
            underlayColor='#99d9f4'>
            <Text style={styles.buttonText}>Add House</Text>
        </TouchableHighlight>
    </View>
```

This is a simple form having two input fields, name and address, along with styling, which we added at the end. Just as in constructor, the state for these two properties was set to an empty string. We update the state with setState once the user fills in the form and pass it to the function onPressButtonPost.

156

You should notice we added a bind in render here. Because we are using ES6 while declaring React components, React no longer autobinds. Therefore we must resolve this by explicitly calling bind in render.

Note   There are other binding patterns to handle this. Here are a few popular ones in React:

1. Binding in render (the one we have used in our application)

    onChange={this.handleChange.bind(this)}

2. Using an arrow function in render

    onPress={e => this.handleChange(e)}

3. Binding in constructor itself

    constructor(props) {

      super(props);

      this.handleChange = this.handleChange.bind(this);

    }

4. Using an arrow function in call property

    handleChange = () => {

      // call this function from render

      // and this.whatever in here works fine.

    };

Next, we created a method onPressButtonPost where the post request is made to a back-end post API.

```
onPressButtonPOST() {
    fetch('https://www.akshatpaul.com/properties', {
        method: 'POST',
        headers: {
        Accept: 'application/json',
        'Content-Type': 'application/json',
            },
        body: JSON.stringify({
            property: {
            name: this.state.name,
            address: this.state.address,
        }
    }),
})
    .then((responseData) => {
        AlertIOS.alert(
            "Created"
        )
    })
    .done();
}
```

Here, we are using the updated values of the name and address properties and making a post request using fetch. Once our request is completed we get an alert box with a Created message.

This was simple. Now let's try our code on a simulator. Once we navigate from the home screen to the add new property screen, we get the form shown in Figure 6-3.

Figure 6-3. *Form to submit a record*

Let's fill in some values to submit to our back-end API (Figure 6-4).

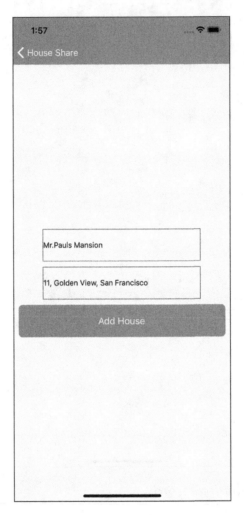

Figure 6-4. *Page to add new house*

Once we submit the data to the back-end API we get the Created message in an alert box (Figure 6-5).

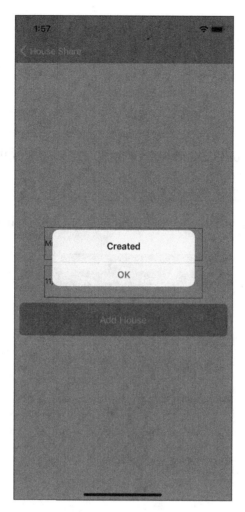

Figure 6-5. *Alert after successful submission*

If you curl this URL, you will get something like this JSON of user-added properties:

```
$curl 'http://www.akshatpaul.com/list-properties'
[
{
name: "Mr. Paul's Mansion",
address: "11, Golden View, San Francisco",
```

```
images: {
thumbnail: "http://hmp.me/ol7"
}
}
]
```

Note   This API shows data submitted by various readers of this book. Your data set might differ.

Refresh the app and go to the List of Properties section (Figure 6-6).

Figure 6-6. *Output showing Mr. Paul's Mansion address*

Note   By default, iOS will block any request that's not encrypted using Secure Sockets Layer (SSL). If you need to fetch from a clear text URL (one that begins with http) you will first need to add an App Transport Security (ATS) exception. If you know ahead of time what domains you will need access to, it is more secure to add exceptions just for those domains; if the domains are not known until runtime you can disable ATS completely. Note, however, that since January 2017, Apple's App Store review requires reasonable justification for disabling ATS.

Summary

This chapter covered various network APIs that are reimplemented from the ground up by the React Native team. You also learned about various options like XMLHttpRequest, WebSocket, and Fetch. Because no application is complete without making server calls, you added this capability into your housing application and learned how to get data from a server, add new records, and save them to a server.

In Chapter 7 we explore Native Bridge for iOS and Android. By using Native Bridge we can access Native iOS or Android APIs from JavaScript.

CHAPTER 7

Native Bridging in React Native

Learn the rules like a pro, so you can break them like an artist.

—Pablo Picasso

So far, you have learned how to build applications using modules and APIs available out of the box with React Native. There are times, however, when an application has to access a native iOS or Android API and its corresponding React Native module is not yet available. Perhaps you will have to reuse some existing bespoke Swift, Kotlin, or Objective-C code with your React Native application. In such scenarios we create something called Native modules, which allow us to write code in the native language of a platform. This chapter covers the following topics:

- What is Native Bridge

- Prerequisite for Native Bridge

- Native Bridge for iOS

- Native Bridge for Android

The concept of Native modules is a bit advanced, but in our experience every production-quality application at some point requires you to delve into a little bit of native programming. Therefore, we consider this an essential skill to know in your journey to becoming a master in React Native.

© Akshat Paul and Abhishek Nalwaya 2019
A. Paul and A. Nalwaya, *React Native for Mobile Development*, https://doi.org/10.1007/978-1-4842-4454-8_7

Native Bridge

To better undersand Native modules, we will create a `Counter` example in Swift for iOS and Java in Android, and this will be used in our React app. This will be a cross-platform example, so the same React code will work in both iOS and Android.

Because many readers of this book might not have worked in Swift or Java, we have tried to keep the use of both these languages very basic, so it should be easily understandable.

Prerequisites for the Example

Because we are writing some code in Native, you should have the following development setup installed on your computer.

- Xcode for running the app for iOS

- Android Studio for running the app for Android

- React Native

We will first create a React Native app with the React Native CLI. We could also use the Expo CLI, but then we would have to eject it to build a Native bridge.

```
$ react-native init CounterNativeModuleApp
$ cd CounterNativeModuleApp
```

This will create the basic structure of the React Native app. It also contains two folders, `iOS` and `android`, which have native code in Objective-C and Java, respectively. We first learn about bridging in iOS, and then use same repo to build for Android.

iOS Native Bridge

We will create a `Counter` class in Swift, which will have a static class variable count and two methods: one for incrementing the count and the other for getting the count value. We will then access this Swift class from JavaScript. Let's start by opening the `CounterNativeModuleApp.xcodeproj` file in the `ios` folder. It should open Xcode with your iOS code.

Create a new file by going to File ➤ New ➤ File and selecting Swift, as shown in Figure 7-1.

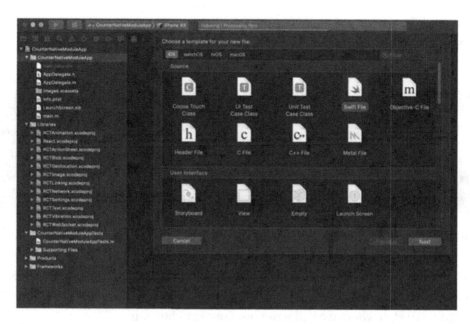

Figure 7-1. *Creating a new file in Swift*

Now give the file the name `Counter` and remember to select
`CounterNativeModuleApp` for the Group setting, as shown in Figure 7-2.

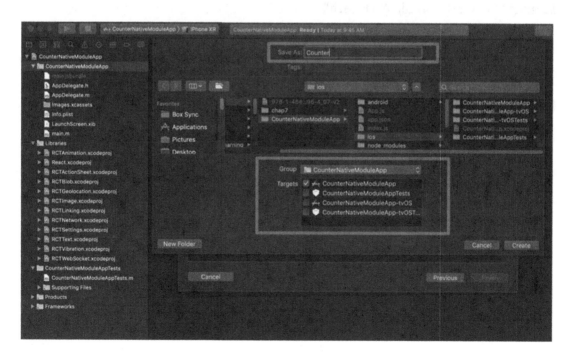

Figure 7-2. *Selecting proper group in Xcode*

As we are writing code in Swift and the repo, which is generated in Objective-C, we need a bridge to communicate between them. Click Create Bridging Header (Figure 7-3).

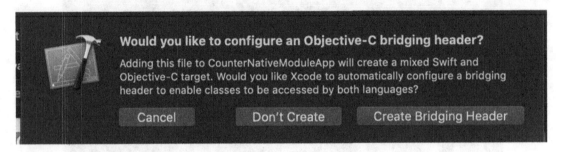

Figure 7-3. *Creating a bridging header*

We can see that two files, `Counter.swift` and `CounterNativeModuleApp-Bridging-Header.h`, are created by Xcode.

`Counter.swift` is where we will write our `Counter` class and `CounterNativeModuleApp-Bridging-Header.h` will have header details. Remember that in a project we have only one bridging header file, so if we add new files, we can reuse this file. Update the following code in the `CounterNativeModuleApp-Bridging-Header.h` file:

```
#import "React/RCTBridgeModule.h"
```

Now let's add a Swift class:

```
import Foundation

@objc(Counter)
class Counter: NSObject {
  @objc
  static var count = 0

  @objc
  func increment() {
    Counter.count += 1
    print("count is \(Counter.count)")
  }

}
```

In the preceding code we have created class `Counter`, which is inherited from `NSObject`. The root class of most Objective-C class hierarchies is `NSObject`, from which subclasses inherit a basic interface to the runtime system and the ability to behave as Objective-C objects.

You can see that we have used `@objc` before a function and class. This will make that class, function, or object available to Objective-C

Note   The `@objc` attribute makes your Swift API available in Objective-C and the Objective-C runtime.

Now create a new file from File ➤ New ➤ File and select Objective-C File. Name the file `Counter` (Figure 7-4).

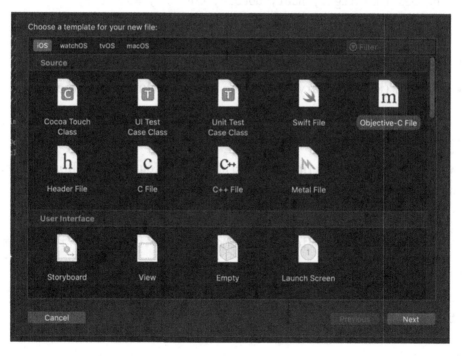

Figure 7-4. *Creating an Objective-C file*

This will create a file `Counter.m`, which will expose the Swift class to React Native:

```
#import "React/RCTBridgeModule.h"
@interface RCT_EXTERN_MODULE(Counter, NSObject)
RCT_EXTERN_METHOD(increment)
@end
```

React Native will not expose any function of `Counter` to React JavaScript unless explicitly done. To do so we can use the `RCT_EXPORT_METHOD()` macro. We therefore have to expose the `Counter` class and `increment` the method to our JavaScript code. Because the Swift object is converted to JSON, there is a type conversion. `RCT_EXPORT_METHOD` supports all standard JSON object types:

- `string (NSString)`
- `number (NSInteger, float, double, CGFloat, NSNumber)`
- `boolean (BOOL, NSNumber)`
- `array (NSArray)` of any types from this list
- `object (NSDictionary)` with string keys and values of any type from this list
- `function (RCTResponseSenderBlock)`

Now let's update the JavaScript code and access this `Counter` class from our React component. To do so, open `App.js` and update it with the following code:

```
import React, {Component} from 'react';
import {StyleSheet, Text, View, NativeModules, Button} from 'react-native';

export default class App extends Component {
  increment = () => {
    NativeModules.Counter.increment();
  }
  render() {
    return (
      <View style={styles.container}>
      <Button
          onPress={this.increment}
```

```
            title="Increment"
            color="#841584"
        />
      </View>
    );
  }
}

const styles = StyleSheet.create({
  container: {
    flex: 1,
    justifyContent: 'center',
    alignItems: 'center',
    backgroundColor: '#F5FCFF',
  }
});
```

We need to import `NativeModule` from `react-native`. The `Counter` method `increment` can be accessed using `NativeModules.Counter.increment()`. We have created a `Button` and clicking on that `button` calls the `increment` method.

Now let's run the app from Xcode by pressing Command + R. Make sure React Native code is running. If it is not, then run `npm start`.

We can see an Increment button and a warning message at the bottom as shown in Figure 7-5. For now, ignore the warning message. We will talk about that later in the chapter.

Figure 7-5. *App running in a simulator*

Now open the Xcode and check the console log. Try clicking the Increment button three times and you will see the output shown in the logs, as displayed in Figure 7-6.

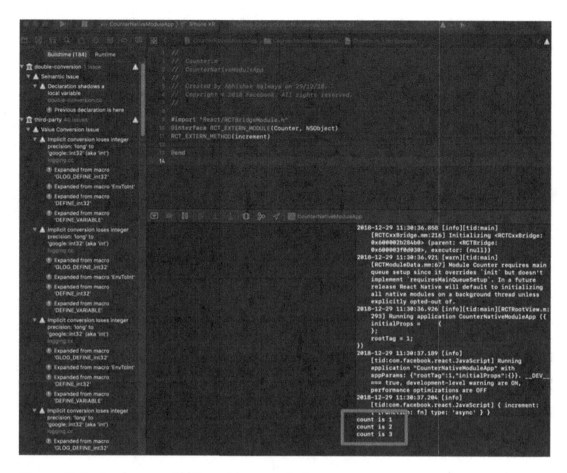

Figure 7-6. *Increment displayed in console log*

We can see that we have called a Swift class method from a JavaScript React component.

Note   Remember, if you change any code in iOS Swift or Objective-C or Android Java, you need to rebuild the project. Only then will changes be reflected.

Now let's fix the warning shown at the bottom of the simulator and in the browser console:

Module Counter requires main queue setup since it overrides 'init' but doesn't implement 'requiresMainQueueSetup'. In a future release React Native will default to initializing all native modules on a background thread unless explicitly opted-out of.

To understand that better, let's understand the thread React Native runs on:

- *Main thread:* Where UIKit works.

- *Shadow queue:* Where the layout happens.

- *JavaScript thread:* Where your JavaScript code is actually running.

- Every native module has its own GCD (Grand Central Dispatch) Queue unless it specifies otherwise.

Now because this Native module will run on a different thread and our main thread is dependent on it, it is showing this warning. To make this code to run on `MainQueue`, open `Counter.swift` and add the following function:

```
@objc
static func requiresMainQueueSetup() -> Bool {
  return true
}
```

Now run the app again. Remember that because we have changed the Swift class, we need to rebuild the code. You will see the app running without the warning now, as shown in Figure 7-7.

Figure 7-7. *Application running without warning*

Now let's add the count value to our React screen. To do so we will add the getCount function to counter.swift and call that method from JavaScript code. We will create this method as a callback.

Note   React Native Bridge is asynchronous, so the only way to pass a result to JavaScript is by using callbacks or emitting events.

Open `counter.swift` and add the `getCount` method:

```swift
import Foundation

@objc(Counter)
class Counter: NSObject {
  @objc
  static var count = 0

  @objc
   func increment() {
    Counter.count += 1
    print("count is \(Counter.count)")
  }

  @objc
  func getCount(_ callback: RCTResponseSenderBlock) {
    callback([NSNull(), Counter.count])
  }

  @objc
  static func requiresMainQueueSetup() -> Bool {
    return true
  }
```

The getCount() method receives a callback parameter that we will pass from your JavaScript code. We have called `callback` with an array of values, which will be exposed in JavaScript. We have passed `NSNull()` as the first element, which we consider an error in callback.

We need to expose this method to `counter.m`:

```objc
#import "React/RCTBridgeModule.h"
@interface RCT_EXTERN_MODULE(Counter, NSObject)
RCT_EXTERN_METHOD(increment)
RCT_EXTERN_METHOD(getCount: (RCTResponseSenderBlock)callback)
@end
```

Let's update the React code to take the count from the getCount method that we just created. Update App.js with following code:

```
import React, {Component} from 'react';
import {StyleSheet, Text, View, NativeModules, Button} from 'react-native';

export default class App extends Component {
  constructor(props) {
    super(props);
    this.state = { count: 0 };
    this.updateCount();
  }
  increment = () => {
    NativeModules.Counter.increment();
    this.updateCount();
    }
  updateCount = () => {
    NativeModules.Counter.getCount( (error, count)=>{
      this.setState({ count: count});
    })
  }
  render() {
    return (
      <View style={styles.container}>
        <Text>Counter from Native Code:</Text>
        <Text>{this.state.count}</Text>
      <Button
          onPress={this.increment}
          title="Increment"
          color="#841584"
        />
      </View>
    );
  }
}
```

```
const styles = StyleSheet.create({
  container: {
    flex: 1,
    justifyContent: 'center',
    alignItems: 'center',
    backgroundColor: '#F5FCFF',
  }
});
```

Rebuild the source code and run the app. You can then see the counter value and when you click Increment, it will increase the count as show, in Figure 7-8.

Figure 7-8. *Application demo in simulator*

Try to refresh the page by pressing Command + R. The count value will be the same and does not reset to 0. If you rebuild the code, however, then the value will be reset to 0.

Native Bridge for Android

In this section we will make the same JavaScript code work with Android. This time we will create a Counter class in java and expose the same functions, increment and getCount, to Javascript.

Open Android Studio (Figure 7-9) and select Open an existing Android Studio project, and then select the android folder inside our CounterNativeModuleApp.

Figure 7-9. *Open the React Native app in Android Studio*

Once the project is opened and it has downloaded all gradle dependency (gradle is the dependency manager of Java), we will create a class Counter. Click Menu ➤ File ➤ New ➤ Java Class. Name the file Counter and then click OK (Figure 7-10).

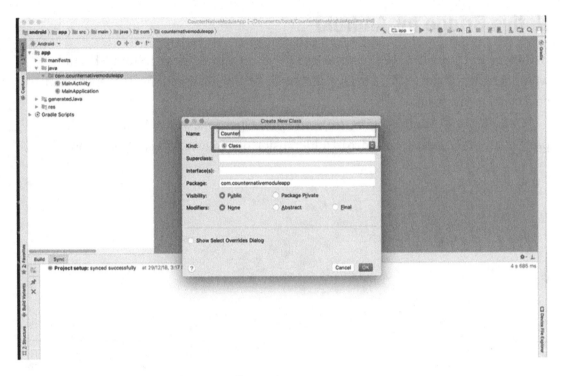

Figure 7-10.   *Creating a Counter class*

Add the following code in Counter.java file:

```
package com.counternativemoduleapp;
import com.facebook.react.bridge.NativeModule;
import com.facebook.react.bridge.ReactApplicationContext;
import com.facebook.react.bridge.ReactContext;
import com.facebook.react.bridge.ReactContextBaseJavaModule;
import com.facebook.react.bridge.ReactMethod;
import com.facebook.react.bridge.Callback;

public class Counter extends ReactContextBaseJavaModule {
    private static Integer count = 0;

    public Counter(ReactApplicationContext reactContext) {
        super(reactContext);
    }

    @ReactMethod
    public void increment() {
```

```
        count++;
        System.out.println(count);

    }

    @ReactMethod
    public void getCount(
            Callback successCallback) {
        successCallback.invoke(null, count);

    }
    @Override
    public String getName() {
        return "Counter";
    }
}
```

We have created the Native module Counter, which is a Java class that is inherited from ReactContextBaseJavaModule. ReactContextBaseJavaModule requires that the function getName is called; this is always implemented. The purpose of this method is to return the string name of the Native module, which represents this class in JavaScript. Here we will call this Counter so that we can access it through React.NativeModules. Counter in JavaScript. Instead of Counter, you could also use a different name.

Not all functions are exposed to JavaScript. To expose a function to JavaScript, a Java method must be annotated using @ReactMethod. The return type of bridge methods is always void, so we create a function increment with @ReactMethod where we have to increase the value of the static variable count and then print the value in the console:

```
@ReactMethod
public void increment() {
    count++;
    System.out.println(count);

}
```

We have also created a getCount function that has callback as a parameter. It returns a callback and passes the value of count.

```
@ReactMethod
public void getCount(
        Callback successCallback) {
    successCallback.invoke(null, count);

}
```

The next step is to register the module, because if a module is not registered it will not be available from JavaScript. To create a file, click Menu ➤ File ➤ New ➤ Java Class. Name the file CustomCounterPackage and then click OK (Figure 7-11).

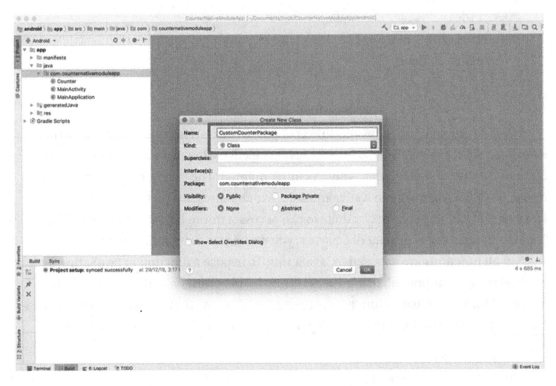

Figure 7-11. *Creating a new Java class*

Now add the following code in CustomCounterPackage:

```
package com.counternativemoduleapp;

import com.facebook.react.ReactPackage;
import com.facebook.react.bridge.NativeModule;
import com.facebook.react.bridge.ReactApplicationContext;
import com.facebook.react.uimanager.ViewManager;
```

```java
import java.util.ArrayList;
import java.util.Collections;
import java.util.List;

public class CustomCounterPackage implements ReactPackage  {
    @Override
    public List<ViewManager> createViewManagers(ReactApplicationContext
    reactContext) {
        return Collections.emptyList();
    }

    @Override
    public List<NativeModule> createNativeModules(
            ReactApplicationContext reactContext) {
        List<NativeModule> modules = new ArrayList<>();

        modules.add(new Counter(reactContext));

        return modules;
    }
}
```

We need to override the createNativeModules function and add the Counter object to the modules array. If this is not added there, it will not be available in JavaScript.

A CustomCounterPackage package needs to be provided in the getPackages method of the MainApplication.java file. This file exists in the android folder in your react-native application directory. Update the following code in android/app/src/main/java/com/CounterNativeModuleApp /MainApplication.java:

```java
package com.counternativemoduleapp;

import android.app.Application;

import com.facebook.react.ReactApplication;
import com.facebook.react.ReactNativeHost;
import com.facebook.react.ReactPackage;
import com.facebook.react.shell.MainReactPackage;
import com.facebook.soloader.SoLoader;
```

```java
import java.util.Arrays;
import java.util.List;
import com.counternativemoduleapp.CustomCounterPackage;

public class MainApplication extends Application implements
ReactApplication {

  private final ReactNativeHost mReactNativeHost = new
  ReactNativeHost(this) {
    @Override
    public boolean getUseDeveloperSupport() {
      return BuildConfig.DEBUG;
    }

    @Override
    protected List<ReactPackage> getPackages() {
      return Arrays.<ReactPackage>asList(
          new MainReactPackage(),
          new CustomCounterPackage()
      );
    }

    @Override
    protected String getJSMainModuleName() {
      return "index";
    }
  };

  @Override
  public ReactNativeHost getReactNativeHost() {
    return mReactNativeHost;
  }

  @Override
  public void onCreate() {
    super.onCreate();
    SoLoader.init(this, /* native exopackage */ false);
  }
}
```

We don't need to change any JavaScript code written in iOS, as we have exposed the same class name and function. If you skipped the iOS section earlier, you need to copy the React JavaScript code from App.js.

Now run the app through Android Studio or from react-native run-android (Figure 7-12).

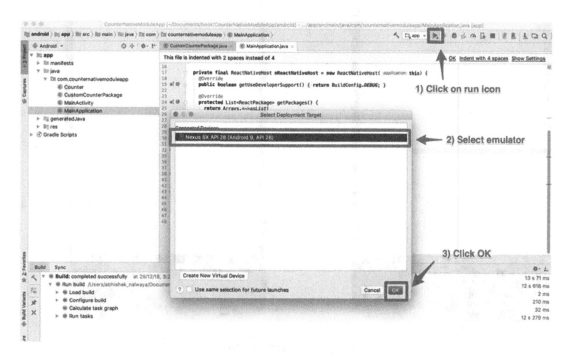

Figure 7-12. *Run the application from Android Studio*

This will launch the Android emulator with the app (Figure 7-13). If you don't find an emulator in the list, you need to download a few by clicking Create New Virtual Device.

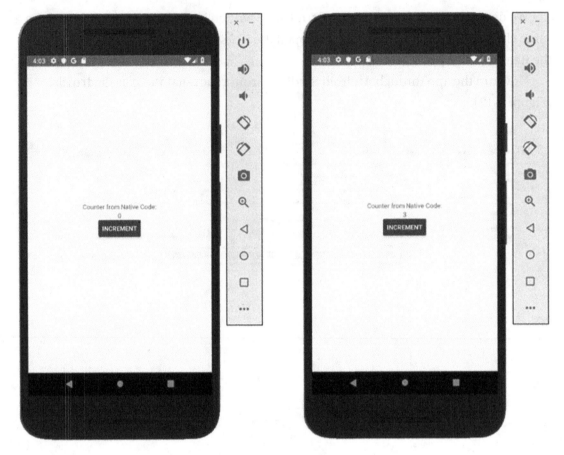

Figure 7-13. *Application running in Android emulator*

We can see the counter change when we click Increment and the JavaScript code is calling the Java code.

Summary

This chapter covered Native Bridge for both iOS and Android. You created a class in Swift and Java and through NativeBridge you were able to access these classes in JavaScript code.

In Chapter 8 you learn about testing in React Native, including type checking using Flow, using Jest with React Native, and understanding how to use snapshot testing.

CHAPTER 8

Testing

Testing is not the point. The point is about responsibility.

—Kent Beck

We do agree with Kent Beck here that testing your code is your responsibility. However, React Native makes it really simple to write tests for your application in comparison to traditional native code for iOS and Android. This chapter covers the following topics:

- Static type checking with Flow

- Jest with React Native

- Snapshot testing

Flow

Flow is a static type checker for JavaScript. It's not essential to use Flow, but it really enhances your development efficiency. Type checking allows you to detect possible issues early by running tests on your project code base. In short, we would say Flow is a productivity module for developers.

To set up Flow for React Native applications, first open your terminal and simply install the following npm module:

```
$ npm install -g flow-bin
```

This will install the flow module globally. Navigate to your React Native application folder and from the root directory, execute the following command:

```
$ flow init
```

This will create a .flowconfig file where all your Flow configurations will reside.

© Akshat Paul and Abhishek Nalwaya 2019
A. Paul and A. Nalwaya, *React Native for Mobile Development*, https://doi.org/10.1007/978-1-4842-4454-8_8

Now, check your application for any errors with the following command:

```
$ flow check
```

```
Found 0 errors
```

Typically, at the beginning of any project, you will find no errors. As you proceed with day-to-day development, however, you can find issues right away and resolve them.

Benefits of Using Flow

Although Flow is a great addition to any React Native application, it's not mandatory. However, we recommend that you include it in your React Native project to experience the following benefits:

- You can code faster without the hassle of running the source code every time to find any issues or bugs.

- It is especially helpful for extensive projects with multiple team members working in parallel. Refactoring can become a nightmare, and Flow helps you focus only on your changes and eliminates worry about breaking other parts of the source code.

- Flow helps developers to understand idiomatic JavaScript. It understands and provides feedback on common JavaScript patterns, which helps developers to create elegent solutions.

- Flow provides real-time feedback, hence saving a great deal of time and improving code quality.

- Flow provides easy integration. As seen earlier, it takes only a few minutes to set up Flow with your project.

Jest

Jest is a unit test framework that is built on top of Jasmine. React Native supports testing of components using Jest (it's also the recommended framework used at Facebook for React Native). Besides React Native, you can also use Jest for other JavaScript projects built using TypeScript, Node, Angular, React for Web, Vue, and many more.

Key featues of the Jest testing framework include the following:

- *Snapshot testing:* Jest allows you to create tests that keep track of large objects. This helps you to write better test cases of UI elements.

- *Zero configuration:* Jest works out of the box and is configuration free.

- *Fast and isolated:* Tests are parallelized by running them in their own processes, which helps maximize performance. Jest runs previous failed tests first and reorganizes the runs based on how long it took to execute the tests.

- *Simple APIs:* Jest makes use of simple conventions that developers are used to. Jest covers the entire toolkit, with updated documentation that is well maintained.

- *Code coverage:* No additional setup is required to pull a built-in code coverage report.

Jest with React Native

Jest is included out of the box with the React Native framework for versions 0.38 and later. You are not required to use Jest, though. Instead, you can also use a Mocha testing framework. When you set up the project initially, create a new project with the following command:

```
$ react-native init jestBasics
```

You will get Jest preloaded, and the following `package.json` code will already be present:

```
"scripts": {
    ...
  "test": "jest"
    ...
},

"devDependencies": {
    ...
    "jest": "24.1.0",
```

```
"react-test-renderer": "16.6.3"

    ...

  },

  "jest": {

     ...

    "preset": "react-native"

     ...

  }
```

There will be a folder created, __tests__, which includes only one file for now, App.js:

```
/**
 * @format
 * @lint-ignore-every XPLATJSCOPYRIGHT1
 */

import 'react-native';
import React from 'react';
import App from '../App';

// Note: test renderer must be required after react-native.
import renderer from 'react-test-renderer';

it('renders correctly', () => {
  renderer.create(<App />);
});
```

If you run yarn test or npm test, your tests will run. Because is there nothing much there yet, you should get the following result:

```
$ yarn test
yarn run v1.9.4
$ jest
 PASS  __tests__/App.js
  ✓ renders correctly (2650ms)

Test Suites: 1 passed, 1 total
Tests:       1 passed, 1 total
Snapshots:   0 total
```

```
Time:        5.756s
Ran all test suites.
```

This was the case if you generated your project using the React Native CLI, but what about Expo? In previous chapters we used Expo to speed up our development process. With Expo the setup process is slightly different because the Expo CLI does not come with Jest out of the box.

For this you would have to set up Jest manually with an include jest-expo, which is not very complicated. You could try this in an existing Expo application you created in a previous chapter or set up a new one.

Navigate to your project folder and add jest-expo to your project using the following command:

```
$ yarn add jest-expo --dev or $ npm i jest-expo --save-dev
```

Open package.json and add the following code:

```
"scripts": {
  "test": "node_modules/.bin/jest"
},
"jest": {
  "preset": "jest-expo"
}
```

Also, create a __test__ folder and add at least one test file with the following sample test:

```
it('works', () => {
  expect(1).toBe(1);
});
```

Open the terminal and run the following code:

```
$ yarn test OR npm test

yarn test
yarn run v1.9.4
$ node_modules/.bin/jest
 PASS  __tests__/Example-test.js
  ✓ works (3ms)
```

```
Test Suites: 1 passed, 1 total
Tests:       1 passed, 1 total
Snapshots:   0 total
Time:        2.288s
Ran all test suites.
  Done in 3.75s.
```

Snapshot Testing with Jest

Snapshotting is a really useful technique in UI development that helps ensure that there are no unexpected changes in the UI during development. With Jest we can capture snapshots of React trees, which help us to compare if there was a breaking change in subsequent changes.

A snapshot test case for a mobile app will render a UI component, take a snapshot, and then compare it to a reference point in the past by storing a snapshot alongside the test case. If the test fails, that means two snapshots did not match due to an unexpected change in the UI. Snapshots should be updated to a new version when a satisfactory UI component is ready.

Let's add our first snapshot test and check the report. Add the following test in the same App.js file. For ease of understanding we are using a project created with the React Native CLI named jestBasics.

```
test("component renders correctly", () => {
  const tree = renderer.create(<App />).toJSON();

  expect(tree).toMatchSnapshot();
});
```

Run the Jest report again with the following command:

```
npm test
```

```
> jestBasics@0.0.1 test /Users/akshatpaul/myapps/react-native-second-edition/
chapter8/jestBasics
> jest

 PASS  __tests__/App.js
  ✓ renders correctly (132ms)
  ✓ component renders correctly (5ms)
```

```
› 1 snapshot written.
Snapshot Summary
 › 1 snapshot written from 1 test suite.

Test Suites: 1 passed, 1 total
Tests:       2 passed, 2 total
Snapshots:   1 written, 1 total
Time:        1.114s, estimated 2s
Ran all test suites.
```

Great! Our test passed and created a snapshot of the render output of our component. This snapshot is saved in a new folder, __snapshots__, which resides inside the __test__ folder. You will find a snapshot file App.js.snap. Open that file if you want to see what's inside a snapshot.

```
// Jest Snapshot v1, https://goo.gl/fbAQLP

exports['component renders correctly 1'] = '
<View
  style={
    Object {
      "alignItems": "center",
      "backgroundColor": "#F5FCFF",
      "flex": 1,
      "justifyContent": "center",
    }
  }
>
  <Text
    style={
      Object {
        "fontSize": 10,
        "margin": 10,
        "textAlign": "center",
      }
    }
  >
```

```
    Welcome to React Native!
  </Text>
  <Text
    style={
      Object {
        "color": "#333333",
        "marginBottom": 5,
        "textAlign": "center",
      }
    }
  >
    To get started, edit App.js
  </Text>
  <Text
    style={
      Object {
        "color": "#333333",
        "marginBottom": 5,
        "textAlign": "center",
      }
    }
  >
    Press Cmd+R to reload,
Cmd+D or shake for dev menu
  </Text>
</View>
`;
```

Do not modify this snapshot. Instead, make some change in your App.js component and see how the snapshot changes and the report fails. Let's make the following change in our styling:

```
const styles = StyleSheet.create({
  container: {
    flex: 1,
    justifyContent: 'center',
```

```
    alignItems: 'flex-start',
    backgroundColor: '#F5FCFF',
  },
  welcome: {
    fontSize: 10,
    textAlign: 'center',
    margin: 10,
  },
  instructions: {
    textAlign: 'center',
    color: '#333333',
    marginBottom: 5,
  },
});
```

Here we have only made one small change in alignItems, changing the setting from center to flex-start. Run the report again and see if the test fails:

npm test

> jestBasics@0.0.1 test /Users/akshatpaul/myapps/react-native-second-edition/
chapter8/jestBasics
> jest

FAIL __tests__/App.js
  ✓ renders correctly (135ms)
  × component renders correctly (9ms)

  ● component renders correctly

    expect(value).toMatchSnapshot()

    Received value does not match stored snapshot "component renders correctly 1".

    - Snapshot
    + Received

```
@@ -1,9 +1,9 @@
  <View
    style={
      Object {
-       "alignItems": "center",
+       "alignItems": "flex-start",
        "backgroundColor": "#F5FCFF",
        "flex": 1,
        "justifyContent": "center",
      }
    }
  18 |    const tree = renderer.create(<App />).toJSON();
  19 |
> 20 |    expect(tree).toMatchSnapshot();
     |                 ^
  21 | });
  22 |

  at Object.toMatchSnapshot (__tests__/App.js:20:16)
```

› 1 snapshot failed.
Snapshot Summary
› 1 snapshot failed from 1 test suite. Inspect your code changes or run
'npm test -- -u' to update them.

```
Test Suites: 1 failed, 1 total
Tests:       1 failed, 1 passed, 2 total
Snapshots:   1 failed, 1 total
Time:        0.886s, estimated 1s
Ran all test suites.
npm ERR! Test failed.  See above for more details.
```

Perfect! Our test failed, and this shows how snapshot testing with Jest really helps during development of a substantial React Native application if one developer makes a change, for example, that might hinder the UI build by someone else.

Summary

Testing is a crucial component in any mobile app development. In this chapter you learned about using Flow to keep your code type checked to assist in detecting issues with your code early and resolving them before they become bugs. Next, you learned about testing with Jest and how to set it up for both React Native CLI apps and those generated using the ExpoCLI. In the end, we introduced the powerful technique of snapshot testing with Jest, which makes building UIs and maintaining them much easier.

Chapter 9 covers iOS and Android app submission to the Apple App Store and Google Play Store, respectively.

Getting Ready for the World

The last 10 percent to launch something takes as much energy as the first 90 percent.

—Rob Kalin

That's a strong quote, but it usually proves quite right. However, when it comes to launching our application with React Native, it is a piece of cake. This chapter covers how you can create a build to distribute your React Native application for both iOS and Android. We also introduce some third-party platforms that are available to make distribution totally stress free. Here are the topics covered in this chapter:

- The Apple and Google Play distribution systems

- Creating a build for iOS or Android

- Beta testing

Apple Developer Account

To create builds for iOS devices for testing or to distribute applications to actual users on the Apple App Store, you must first create and pay for an Apple Developer Account. An individual developer account costs around US$99 and works perfectly for independent developers, or even for developers who are part of a small organization. However, if your company policy requires you to be a member of a team, then your company can go open Enterprise account. Table 9-1 lists the differences so you can determine what works best for your organization.

Table 9-1. *Selecting Your Options*

	Only Apple ID	Apple Developer Program	Enterprise Program
Xcode developer tools	✓	✓	✓
Xcode beta releases	✓	✓	✓
Test on device	✓	✓	✓
Developer forums	✓	✓	✓
OS beta releases	✕	✓	✓
Advanced app capabilities	✕	✓	✓
Code-level support	✕	✓	✓
Distribution outside Apple App Store	✕	✓	✓
App Store distribution	✕	✓	✕
App Store connect	✕	✓	✕
Safari extensions	✕	✓	✕
Offering custom apps	✕	✓	✕
Distribution of custom apps to your employees	✕	✓	✕
Distribution of your proprietary apps to your employees	✕	✕	✓
Cost	Free	US$99 (annually)	US$299 (annually)

To create your Apple Developer Account, visit `https://developer.apple.com/`.

Google Play Console

In the case of Android, you explicitly do not need to have a paid account from Google Play at the time of development or testing. However, eventually when you have to distribute your application (i.e., publish it to the Google Play Store) you would have to pay a one-time registration fee of US$25. However, this will only be required toward the end of the chapter if you wish to publish your app to the Play Store.To learn more about the Google Play Console visit `https://play.google.com/apps/publish/`.

iOS Build Process

To get ready, we must set up our Apple Developer Profile. Apple has a specific way of setting up certificates, IDs, and profiles. Not to worry; we'll learn about them all by setting them up for our React Native app. Once you have your paid Developer account, log in into `https://developer.apple.com/`. You'll have two options, as shown in Figure 9-1.

Figure 9-1. *Apple Developer console*

The first option is Certificates, Identifiers & Profiles and the second one is App Store Connect. The App Store is the place where we will upload our application build to be submitted to Apple for publishing our app to the App Store and also for beta testing our application using TestFlight.

Open the Certificates, Identifiers & Profiles page, select Development on the left, and then click the plus (+) button on the right to begin the development and distribution certificate process (Figure 9-2).

Figure 9-2. *Beginning the development and distribution process*

You will then have the option to create either a development or distribution certificate (Figure 9-3).

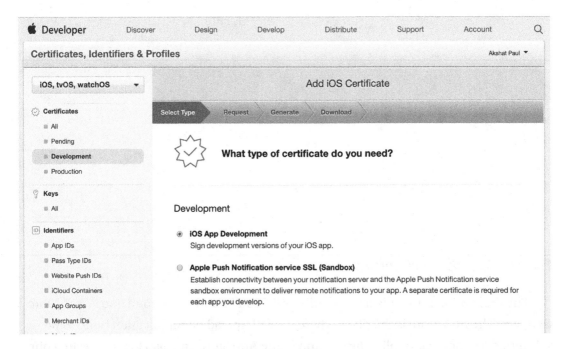

Figure 9-3. *Selecting development and distribution certificates*

We will require both because we plan to publish our application to the App Store and the process is the same for both. Select iOS App Development and continue to the next step. There you will see instructions how to generate the certificate on your Mac machine, which will be then uploaded. For this you will make use of the Keychain utility.

Create a CSR File

In the Applications folder on your Mac, open the Utilities folder and launch Keychain Access. From the Keychain Access drop-down menu, select Keychain Access ➤ Certificate Assistant ➤ Request a Certificate from a Certificate Authority. In the Certificate Information window, enter the following information:

1. In the User Email Address field, enter your e-mail address.

2. In the Common Name field, create a name for your private key (e.g., John Doe Dev Key).

3. The CA Email Address field should be left empty.

4. In the Request is group, select Saved to disk.

Click Continue within Keychain Access to complete the CSR generating process. Once this is complete, click Continue and you see an option to upload the CSR file in your developer portal (Figure 9-4).

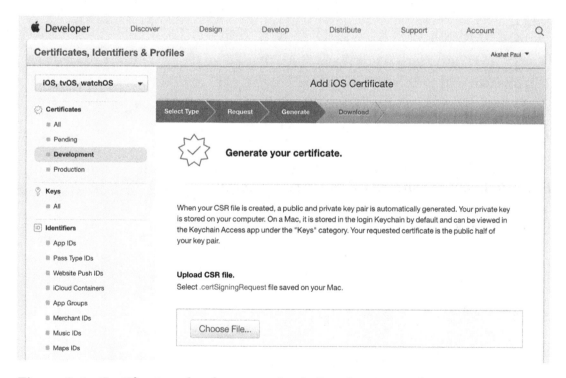

Figure 9-4. *Certificate upload page on Apple Developer portal*

Once the CSR file is uploaded, click Continue. At the last step you will have the option to download the certificate. Double-click it and it will get loaded in your Keychain.

Next, follow the same steps and set up distribution certification. On successful completion you can check both your installed certificates in Keychain ➤ My Certifications.

We next create an App ID that will be unique for every application. Under Identifiers, select App IDs and then click the plus (+) button (Figure 9-5).

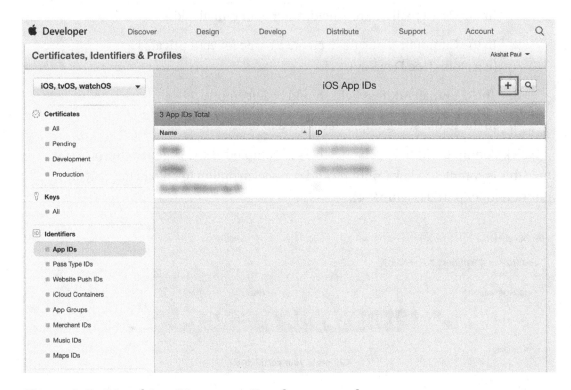

Figure 9-5. *List of App ID page on Developer portal*

That will open the screen shown in Figure 9-6.

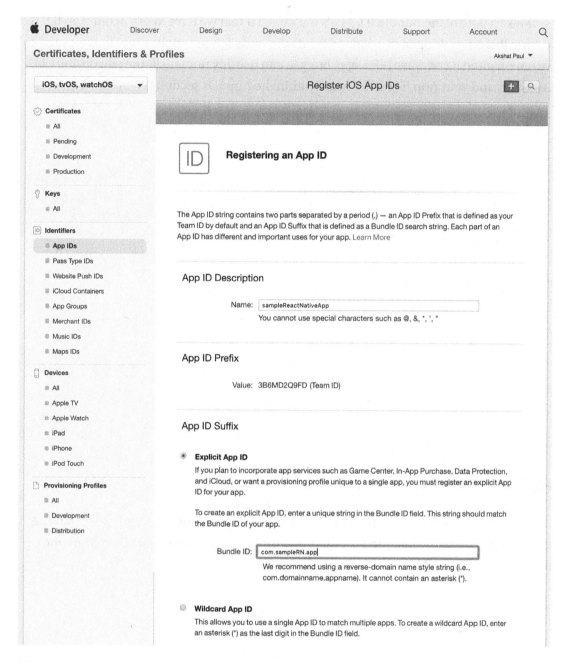

Figure 9-6. *Registering an App ID in the Apple Developer portal*

Make a note of the Bundle ID, as it's the same ID that we have to use in our App ID. We will use this once we open our code to create the build for our application. In our example we have named it `com.sampleRN.app`, but you can use any nomenclature you desire. Click Continue, and your App ID will be listed within the App IDs section (Figure 9-7).

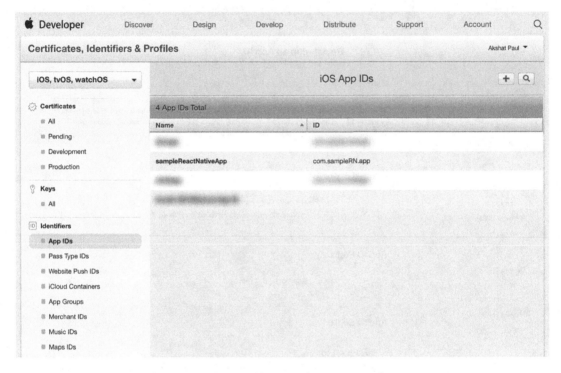

Figure 9-7. *App ID shown in the Apple Developer portal*

Next, we create a Development and Distribution profile for the `sampleReactNative` application. Scroll down to the Provisioning Profiles section and select Development, then click the plus (+) button (Figure 9-8).

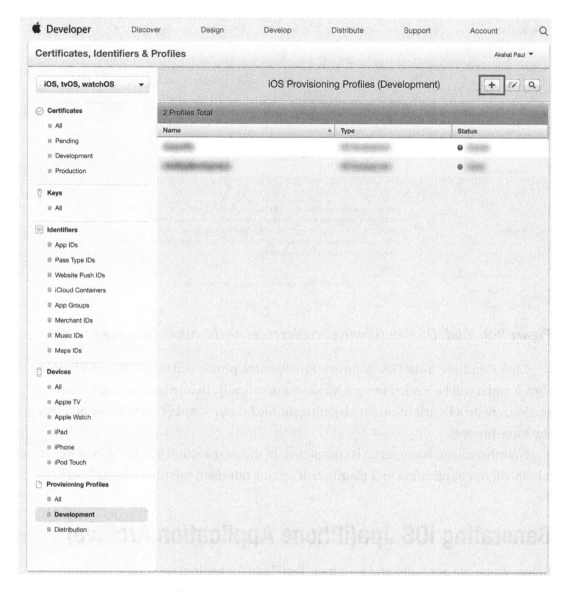

Figure 9-8. *iOS Provisioning Profiles list page in the Apple Developer portal*

Select the appropriate App ID from the drop-down list. In our case it will be the App ID we created in the previous section for our `sampleReactNative` app (Figure 9-9).

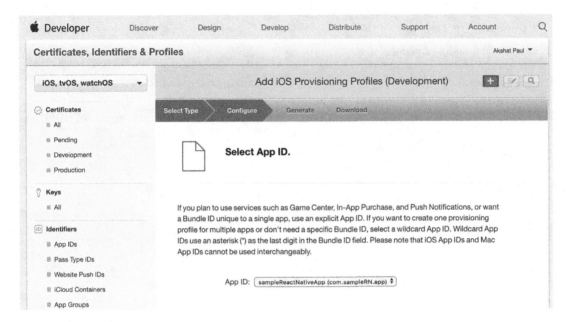

Figure 9-9. *Add iOS Provisioning Profiles page on the Apple Developer portal*

Click Continue. Your Development Provisioning profile will be generated. Double-click it and it will be loaded in your Xcode automatically. Before proceeding to the next section, create a Distribution Provisioning profile for our `sampleReactNative` app using the same process.

Now that all our basic setup is completed, in the next section you learn how we create a build for our application and distribute it among our team members using TestFlight.

Generating iOS .ipa(iPhone Application Archive)

Before we create our build and host it on TestFlight for testing, we should load our source code in Xcode. From the root of your React Native source code, navigate to the appropriate folder and click the Xcode project file (Figure 9-10).

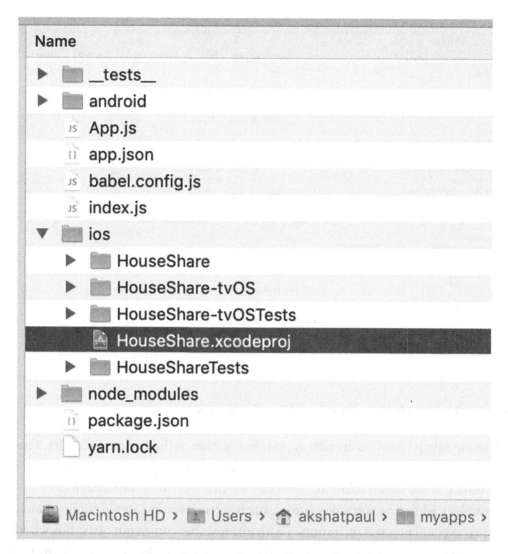

Figure 9-10. *Folder structure of iOS project*

Double-click this to load your application in Xcode. Click the General tab for the application to add the settings shown in Figure 9-11.

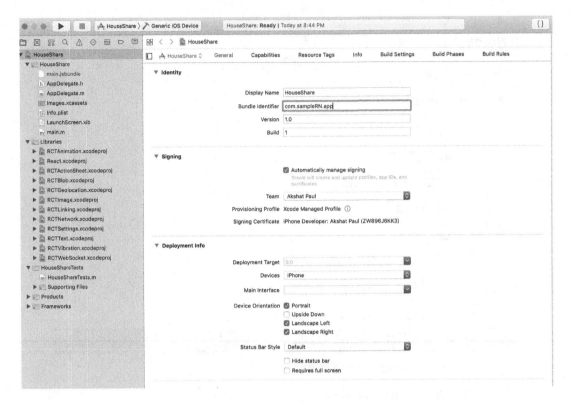

Figure 9-11. *Xcode General tab settings for the project*

Use the App ID you had created in previous section as the Bundle Identifier. This has to be same, as mentioned in the Developer console, and unique for every application you create. It is essentially a unique identifier for your app in Apple's system.

Next, let's add some app icons and a launch screen for our sample application. It's fine to keep your launch screen simple, with just text that comes out of the box when you initialize a React Native application. However, we must add all types of icons for our build to be successful and submitted to Apple for both App Store release and testing with TestFlight.

To add icons to your application, select Images.xcassets ➤ AppIcon folder from the project directory from Xcode (Figure 9-12).

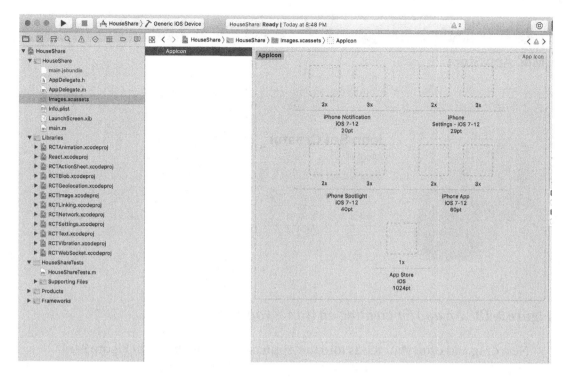

Figure 9-12. *Icon image set screen in Xcode*

The icons shown here represent the same icon for your application to be used at different places; in short, they represent your application icon in various sizes. We won't get into a tutorial here about how to create these icons, because that's a designer's area of expertise. For our work, we can use some application—we suggest downloading Icon Set Creator for your Macintosh—to generate all sizes of icons for iOS devices (Figure 9-13). There are many online sites that can help you perform the same task.

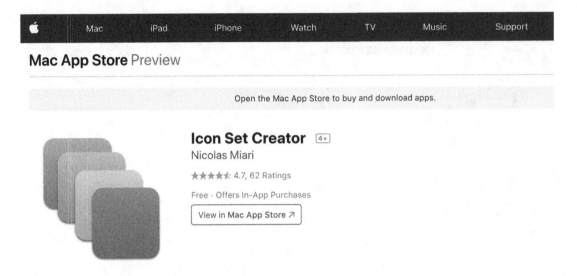

Figure 9-13. *An app for creating an icon set on Mac*

Next drag and drop your icons into the AppIcon pane, as shown in Figure 9-14.

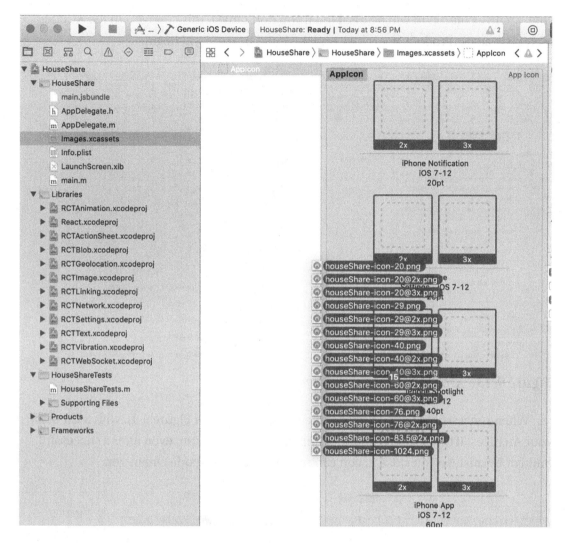

Figure 9-14. *Icon image set screen in Xcode*

Once this is done, you will see all your icons automatically set up and you're ready for the next step, which is setting up your launch screen.

Select LaunchScreen.xib to add or modify the launch screen for your application. In our sample application, we will keep the same default launch screen because it won't break our build or stop us from uploading it. However, for a real-world application that is supposed to be published to the App Store, it is better to have a proper launch screen.

Next, let's create our build, which is actually done using the Archive command. Before we create the build, please select Generic iOS Device as the target, as shown in Figure 9-15. The reason for changing this from a simulator to Generic iOS Device is that

your Archive command will be disabled if you don't make this change. On the XCode
menu bar, select Product ➤ Archive and the build process will begin.

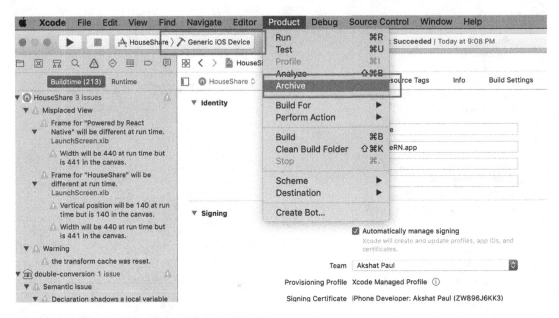

Figure 9-15. *Xcode archive generation*

When successfully built, you'll get the window shown in Figure 9-16 with a list of all
your Archives. If this window does not appear for some reason, even after a successful
build or by mistake you close it, you can reopen it. This is Xcode Organizer.

Figure 9-16. *Xcode Organizer*

Click Distribute App and you will be presented with a few options. Select iOS App Store and after few steps your ipa will be ready to be uploaded to App Store Connect (Figure 9-17).

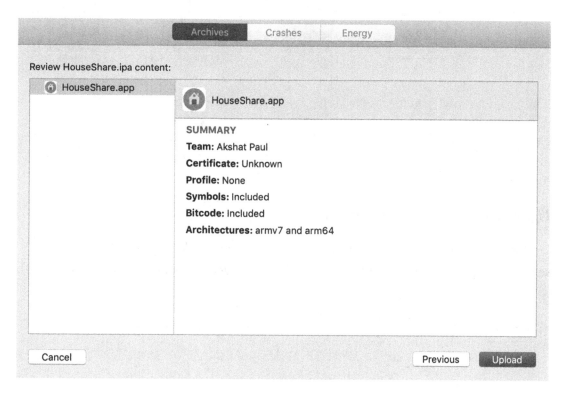

Figure 9-17. *Xcode Organizer detail screen*

Before clicking Upload, you need to first create the application on the App Store Connect. Go to https://developer.apple.com/account and select the App Store Connect icon or visit https://appstoreconnect.apple.com/. There you'll find several options. Select My Apps, as shown in Figure 9-18.

Figure 9-18. *App Store Connect home page*

Inside My Apps you will see all your iOS applications. Click the plus (+) button and select New App to create new App Store app for our React Native application (Figure 9-19).

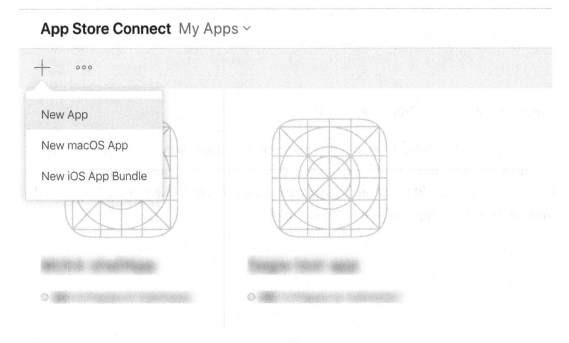

Figure 9-19. *App Store Connect create new app*

Once selected, the form displayed in Figure 9-20 will appear.

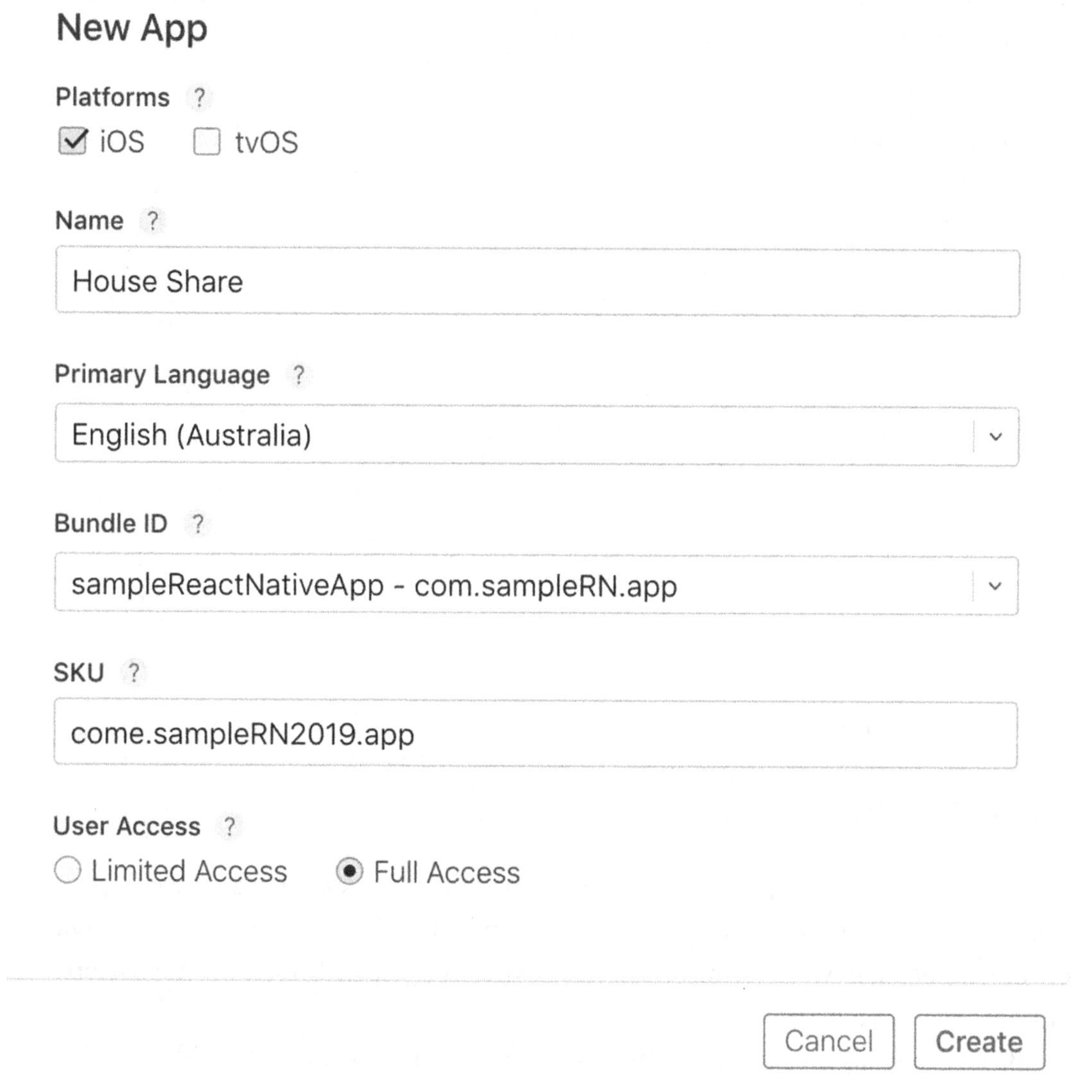

New App

Platforms ?

☑ iOS   ☐ tvOS

Name ?

House Share

Primary Language ?

English (Australia)   ⌄

Bundle ID ?

sampleReactNativeApp - com.sampleRN.app   ⌄

SKU ?

come.sampleRN2019.app

User Access ?

◯ Limited Access   ⦿ Full Access

Cancel   Create

Figure 9-20. *App Store Connect form to create a new app*

Fill it out with the proper details for your application. You can select the appropriate Bundle ID from the drop-down list. A SKU has to be added, which can be different from the Bundle ID. This SKU is not visible to App Store users. For user access, if you have created any specific user group already you can select it. If not, select Full Access, especially if this is your first application.

Click Create and your empty app will be created on App Store Connect. Go back to Xcode and continue where we left off. Click Upload and shortly your application build will be uploaded on App Store Connect (Figure 9-21).

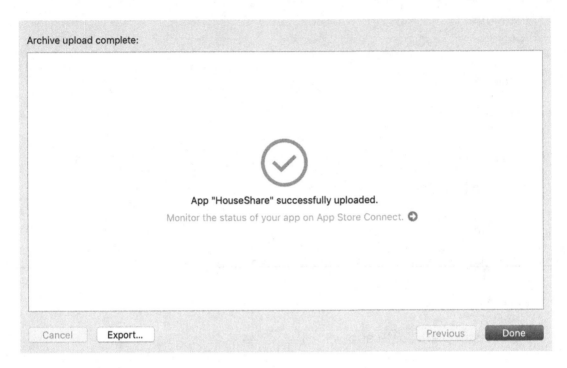

Figure 9-21. *Organizer success screen*

You can check your application build on App Store Connect in a few. From App Store Connect, you can submit your application to Apple for review. After a successful review of your application without issues and errors, your app will be live on the Apple App Store for users in two to five days.

Before you publish your application for end users, it must be thoroughly tested. This process is called beta testing and can be achieved using TestFlight.

Generating Android .apk(Android application package)

Just like Apple, Google expects all Android apps to be signed with a certificate before they get installed on a device either for testing or publishing in the Google Play Store.

To begin this process, first navigate to the folder where your Java Development Kit (JDK) is installed. In the case of Macintosh, if you are not sure where your JDK is installed, type the following command in your terminal:

```
$ /usr/libexec/java_home
```

This will print the path to the jdk folder. Navigate to that directory and type the following command:

```
$ sudo keytool -genkey -v -keystore my-release-key.keystore -alias my-key-alias -keyalg RSA -keysize 2048 -validity 10000
```

When you execute this command, it will ask few questions and require a password to be set for your keys. Please remember the password because it will be used later when applying these settings for your React Native application.

Copy the my-release-key.keystore file in the android/app directory in your React Native application folder (Figure 9-22).

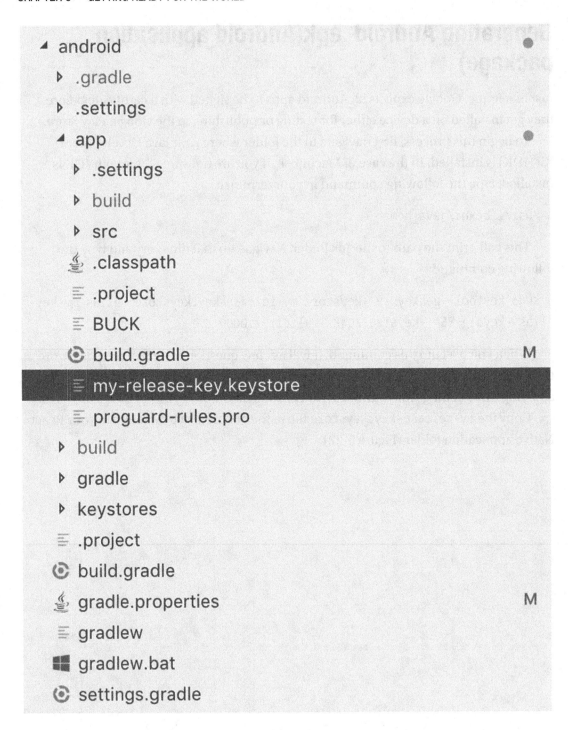

Figure 9-22. *Android folder structure of app*

Note   Always make sure to keep your keys private and never commit in the project directory.

Next, we need to add some configurations in two files. First open android/gradle. properties and add the following settings:

```
MYAPP_RELEASE_STORE_FILE=my-release-key.keystore
MYAPP_RELEASE_KEY_ALIAS=my-key-alias
MYAPP_RELEASE_STORE_PASSWORD=*****
MYAPP_RELEASE_KEY_PASSWORD=*****
```

As mentioned earlier, provide the password you set when you were generating your keys.

Next, open android/app/build.gradle. In signingConfigs ➤ release section, add the following config:

```
signingConfigs {
    release {
        if (project.hasProperty('MYAPP_RELEASE_STORE_FILE')) {
            storeFile file(MYAPP_RELEASE_STORE_FILE)
            storePassword MYAPP_RELEASE_STORE_PASSWORD
            keyAlias MYAPP_RELEASE_KEY_ALIAS
            keyPassword MYAPP_RELEASE_KEY_PASSWORD
        }
    }
}
```

In the same file inside the buildTypes ➤ release section, add the following config:

```
buildTypes {
    release {
        ...
        signingConfig signingConfigs.release
    }
}
```

Finally, to generate an apk, go to the `android` folder in your React Native application and execute the following command:

```
$ gradlew assembleRelease
```

This will generate the apk build that can you can find at `android/app/build/outputs/apk/release/app-release.apk`. This apk can be distributed to users and submitted to the Google Play Store.

Beta Testing with TestFlight

TestFlight is a utility that is included when you set up your Apple Developer Account. It allows you to invite users to test your application, provide you with feedback, and provide you with valuable test information like crashes, and so on.

Each build is active for 90 days and you can invite up to 25 internal testers (which does not require App Store review) and up to 10,000 external testers, which is only applicable after App Store review.

Let's also set up our sample React Native application for TestFlight. The process is pretty simple. Inside App Store Connect, select your application and click the TestFlight tab (Figure 9-23).

Figure 9-23. *App Store Connect TestFlight tab*

You will see the recently uploaded build available. It will mention missing compliance. Under App Information, select Test Information from the menu pane. Click the Missing Compliance message again and click Start Internal Testing.

You can invite up to 25 users to participate in internal testing. To add users, return to the App Store Connect home screen and select Users and Access. From there, you can add your testing users and segregate them into groups if required.

Your testers would have to install the TestFlight application from the Apple App Store to access the build, which will be installed separately on your iOS device.

TestFlight is a good option, but it is limited to only iOS device testing. Besides TestFlight we would recommend TestFairy and HockeyApp as alternatives that can be used for both iOS and Android. Whereas TestFairy is a paid utility, HockeyApp is completely free (at the time of this writing).

Summary

In this chapter we finally reached the end of the development cycle for a mobile application, creating a build that can be tested by users and submitted to the Apple App Store or the Google Play Store. You learned about the signing process for both systems: Whereas Apple has specific steps in its signing process, the Google Android process is fairly quick. Both, though, are designed to keep the rights and devices of users from being misused. You also learned about beta testing with TestFlight and some other popular options.

CHAPTER 10

The Ecosystem: Extending React Native

Civilization advances by extending the number of operations which we can perform without thinking about them.

—Alfred North Whitehead

If you have come this far, you can proudly say you have become a React Native developer. In this final chapter you learn how expedite your React Native development by using some very useful, stable, and popular libraries. These are designed to make your life a bit easier and help you create your apps faster. This chapter covers the following topics:

- Popular React Native libraries
- Community, Help, and where to go from here

Popular React Native Libraries

From the time of its inception the React Native ecosystem has grown by leaps and bounds. The React Native community is vibrant and exceptionally productive: With every passing week, something new is always coming up to untangle the complications of development. By the time you have reached this chapter and we have completed this book, a lot more must have happened (later in this chapter we share ways to stay updated with the community). However, this chapter provides a curated list of libraries organized based on categories to help you increase the velocity of your React Native development.

© Akshat Paul and Abhishek Nalwaya 2019

A. Paul and A. Nalwaya, *React Native for Mobile Development*, https://doi.org/10.1007/978-1-4842-4454-8_10

UI

Styled-components

Styled-components allows you to write actual CSS code to style your components. It removes the mapping between components and styles: Using components as a low-level styling construct makes it easy. See `https://github.com/styled-components/styled-components`.

Lottie-react-native

Lottie is a mobile library for Android and iOS that parses Adobe After Effects animations exported as JSON with bodymovin (an After Effects extension to export anmations for the Web) and renders them natively on mobile platforms. Access the `Lottie` mobile library here: `https://github.com/react-native-community/lottie-react-native`.

React-native-vector-icons

This library is perfect for buttons, logos, and navigation and tab bars. It is easy to extend, style, and integrate into your project. It provides customizable icons for React Native with support for NavBar/TabBar/Toolbar, image source, and full styling. See `https://github.com/oblador/react-native-vector-icons`.

Forms

Formik

Formik is a simple library that helps you with the three parts that make forms in React complicated: getting values in and out of form state, validation and error messages, and handling form submission. See `https://github.com/jaredpalmer/formik`.

Redux-form

`Redux-form` is the most convenient way to manage a form state in Redux. To make use of this module you must have some idea about the Redux state container and higher order components. See `https://github.com/erikras/redux-form/`.

Type Checking and Linting

ESLint

ESLint is an open source project that has as its ultimate goal to provide a pluggable linting utility for JavaScript. There are many popular ESLint configurations available from popular projects that can import for your application while also creating new custom linting rules based on your requirement. See `https://eslint.org/`.

Prop-types

Prop-types is a library that helps in runtime type checking for React props and similar objects. See `https://www.npmjs.com/package/prop-types`.

Flow

Flow is a static type checker for JavaScript that helps identify problems with your code early instead of guessing and checking. `Flow` provides real-time feedback as you code and make your changes. See `https://flow.org/`.

Testing

Jest

Jest is a testing framework that is simple to use and integrate with your React Native application. It comes out of the box with React Native versions 0.38 and above. Jest also allows for snapshot testing, which is a brilliant way to manage changes in the UI. See `url: https://jestjs.io/`.

Enzyme

Enzyme is a testing tool that was created and open sourced by Airbnb. It supports tons of features like shallow rendering, full DOM rendering, and static rendered markup. It is a great add-on, along with Jest. Enzyme APIs are intuitive and flexible as they imitate Jquery APIs for DOM manipulations. See `https://github.com/airbnb/enzyme`.

Chai

Chai is an assertion testing library based on test-driven and behavior-driven development. Just like Enzyme, Chai also enahances other testing frameworks. See `https://www.chaijs.com/`.

Mocha

Mocha is a JavaScript testing framework that helps make asynchronous testing simple. Mocha runs test serially and provides accurate reporting, while mapping uncaught exceptions to the correct test cases. See `https://mochajs.org/`.

Interacting with APIs and Back End

Axios

Axios is an HTTP client for JavaScript that helps make HTTP requests to REST endpoints and perform CRUD operations. Axois supports Promise API, intercept request and response, helps transform request and response data, and has many more features. See `https://github.com/axios/axios`.

Apollo

If you plan to use GraphQL you will end up using Apollo, which is an implementation of GraphQL that helps manage data in the cloud. Apollo includes two open source libraries for the client and server, in addition to developer tools that provide everything you need to run a graph API in production with confidence. See `https://www.apollographql.com/docs/react/recipes/react-native.html`.

React-native-firebase

React-native-firebase is a collection of official React Native modules connecting you to Firebase services; each module is a lightweight JavaScript layer connecting you to the native Firebase SDKs for both iOS and Android. See `https://github.com/invertase/react-native-firebase`.

Routing

React Router

React Router is a collection of navigational components that compose declaratively with your application. Whether you want to have URLs that can be bookmarked for your web app or a composable way to navigate in React Native, React Router works perfectly. See `https://reacttraining.com/react-router`.

React Navigation

React Navigation was born from the React Native community's need for an extensible yet easy-to-use navigation solution written entirely in JavaScript (so you can read and understand all of the source), on top of powerful native primitives. See `https://reactnavigation.org/`.

Utilities

Lodash

Lodash is a JavaScript library that provides utility functions for common programming tasks using the functional programming paradigm. Lodash is the most commonly used library in any application and it is very popular in the JavaScript world. See `https://lodash.com/docs/4.17.11`.

Ramda

Ramda is a library designed specifically for a functional programming style, one that makes it easy to create functional pipelines and never mutates user data. See `https://ramdajs.com/`.

Moment

`Moment.js` is brilliant for managing dates in JavaScript, which is something you will always stumble on when developing an application. See `https://momentjs.com/`.

Reselect

Reselect is a simple "selector" library with Redux. Having key features like selectors can compute derived data, allowing Redux to store the minimal possible state. Selectors are efficient; a selector is not recomputed unless one of its arguments changes. They are also composable, and they can be used as input to other selectors. See `https://github.com/reduxjs/reselect`.

Validate.js

Validation is part of any application. `Validate.js` serves this purpose by providing a declarative way of validating JavaScript objects. With `Validate.js`, validation constraints can be declared in JSON and shared between clients and the server. See `https://validatejs.org/`.

React-native-device-info

This is a simple library, and as its name suggests, it provides device information for React Native for iOS and Android. It has a long list of APIs to provide in-depth information about the device on which an application is running. See `https://github.com/rebeccahughes/react-native-device-info`.

Where to Get Help

This section provides some suggestions on where to get help in the React Native community.

React Native Repository

The React Native repository is maintained by a full-time Facebook React Native core team, but there is huge community that is always contributing to keeping this framework stable. You can always raise an issue if you find one with the framework in the GitHub repository, and there you can also find solutions to past issues. See `https://github.com/facebook/react-native/issues`. To report a bug in the framework you can use the bug report format available at `https://github.com/facebook/react-native/issues/new?template=bug_report.md`.

Stack Overflow

Stack Overflow is a place where people across the React Native community help each other. You can post questions and get answers pretty quickly. You can also help fellow developers as you proceed in your journey toward becoming an expert in React Native (or any other technology). By giving answers to various questions, your score on Stack Overflow increases, which is a kind of motivation for helping others. Many developers actually boast about their Stack Overflow stats. See `https://stackoverflow.com/questions/tagged/react-native?sort=frequent` for a list of exisiting questions on React Native. To ask a question with a React Native tag, go to `https://stackoverflow.com/questions/ask?tags=react-native`.

Stay Updated with React Native

You should also stay in tune with the latest happenings in React Native with the official documentation available at `https://github.com/facebook/react-native-website`. The official blog of React Native maintained at `https://facebook.github.io/react-native/blog/` will keep you updated on what is new. You can also connect with the official React Native Twitter account, which keeps updated with both React Native and Reactjs. See `https://twitter.com/reactjs`.

React Native Communities

Sometimes if you don't get an answer quickly on GitHub issues or Stack Overflow, it's a good idea to get in touch with the larger community instantly. For that you can join the React Discord channel and connect with fellow developers. Incidentally, it's not necessary for you have questions; you can always share your discovery or maybe your next open source React Native project. This is a good way to get some visibility. See `https://discordapp.com/invite/0ZcbPKXt5bZjGY5n`.

Another way to interact with the React Native developer community is to be part of various online groups and forums. Here are a few recommended ones you can join:

- *React Native Spectrum:* `https://spectrum.chat/react-native`

- *React Native Facebook group:* `https://www.facebook.com/groups/react.native.community`

- *Expo forum:* `https://forums.expo.io/`

Knowledge

Besides the official React Native blog, there are some amazing posts written on other blogs by community members that can further enhance your knowledge. Here are two recommended ones:

- *DevTo community:* `https://dev.to/t/reactnative`
- *React Native on Medium:* `https://medium.com/tag/react-native`

Discussions and Proposals

React Native, although very powerful, is still a young framework and its core team is always looking for great proposals, improvements, and discussions. Be part of this problem-solving effort and contribute to this thriving community. You can do this by following the formal channel at `https://github.com/react-native-community/discussions-and-proposals`.

Summary

Now we have reached the end of our book and our last summary. In this chapter we provided information about various React Native libraries that can expedite our development time and give access to the enormous treasure trove of features built over time by the React Native community. You also learned about how to stay updated on this fast-moving framework by getting information from the right sources.

Although you have learned a lot during the course of this book, to truly master this topic you have to keep practicing and creating apps. There is no better way to become an expert at a technology than learning on your own in a real-world scenario. You can contribute to the developer community by creating a module that still does not exist or by contributing to existing open source React Native repos. We are very excited about React Native, just like you, and look forward to seeing your work making a mark in the mobile development and React Native world.

Index

A

Alert method, 127, 128
Android Virtual Devices (AVDs), 33
Animations, 99–101
Apple Developer Account
  Beta testing with test flight, 222
  generating android apk, 219–222
  generating iOS ipa
    App Store connect, 215–218
    icons, 211, 213
    settings, 210
    Xcode archive generation, 214
    Xcode Organizer, 214
    Xcode project file, 208, 209
  iOS build process, 201
    add provisioning
      profiles, 207, 208
    App ID, 204–206
    certificate uploaded on Apple
      Developer portal, 204
    create development and
      distribution process, 202
    Keychain Access, 203
    Select development, 202
  populated list with options, 200
AsyncStorage, 116, 119–123

B

Beta testing, 218, 222–223

C

catch() method, 148
Communication, 141
  fetch, 143
  server
    get data, 145–148
    saving data
      (*see* Data saving, server)
  WebSocket, 142, 143
  XMLHttpRequest, 142
componentDidMount() method, 121, 148

D, E

Data saving, server
  AddNewProperty, 153–155
  Addproperty page, 149
  alert box message, 160, 161
  back-end API, 149
  list of properties, 162
  navigation route, 152
  post request, 158
  setState, 156
  simulator, 158
Debugging, React Native, 42
  in Chrome, 43, 44
  FPS Monitor, 45
  inspect element, 46, 47
  reload option, 43
  in Safari, 44

© Akshat Paul and Abhishek Nalwaya 2019
A. Paul and A. Nalwaya, *React Native for Mobile Development*, https://doi.org/10.1007/978-1-4842-4454-8

F